The Coming of Islam in Bilad al-Sudan

By: Ini-Herit Shawn P

© Kofi Piesie ReSearch Team. © Same Tree Different Branch

Kofi Piesie/Mossi Warrior Clan
Copywright 2020 by Kofi Piesie Research Team

All rights reserved. No part of this book may be reproduced or transmitted in any form or by any means, electronic or mechanical, including photocopying, recording, or by any information storage and retrieval systems without the written permission of the publisher.

Printed in the United States of America

Table of Contents

Acknowledgement

Forward - Ankh West

Introduction

Chapter One - Hypothesis

Chapter Two - The Coming of Islam & The Role of Syncretism

Chapter Three - The Meaning of Jihad & It's Use in Bilad al-Sudan

Chapter Four - The Role Race & Slavery Played Among The Muslim World

Chapter Five - The Claim - Did Islam Come In Peace? A response to Lord Abba

Chapter Six - The Spread of Islam Meant Controlling The Trade

Chapter Seven - Bilad al Bidan White Rule in Ancient West Africa

Overall

Bibliography

Truth is the first victim of war…African Proverb
Dedicated to every person who has lived and died dedicating their lives to the ideas and qualities of Truth in the pursuit to expand, advance, mold, cherish and protect, TRUTH

Acknowledgement

To my family & friends I dedicate this work to you and may this open the eyes of the blind and the minds or the closed who has been lead astray by ideology and misinformation which has crippled the community we attempt to protect and serve. In every addition of a book I seek to inspire the lost as Ini-herit Khalfani means 'He who brings back the lost shall lead'. This is my attempt to reach those some see as lost and bring them back to their center which has been forgotten for hundreds of years due to a mass kidnapping, enslavement, colonialism, and much more… May this work inspire the next generation as they shall build on this correct the mistakes I may have made and move us forward in their moment in history. To my Teams I appreciate the push forward and the opportunity to work along side of great researchers, scholars, and activist who pour their hearts in trying to right so many wrongs and educate the hearts and minds of the people. To the reader of this text stay focused this is your time right here in this moment.

Created and shot by : **Rich Allela** Photography assistant : **Ella Seling**

Forward

"Truth is a continuous examination, and Fact always supersedes belief." Author and Atheist — Yosef A.A. Ben-Jochannan

In Africa's early exploration or exploitation, natural resources, sacred text, and statues held in observance of our indigenous African ancestors became idols. They were considered evil by European and Muslim invaders. When the Africans worshiped the natural world in deities and gods, this was deemed savage. The hordes of invading empires forced their culture on the African way of life. According to Islamic historiography, Muhimid sent ambassadors with letters to Munzir ibn Sawa, governor of the Persian Sasanian Empire of historical Bahrain, Muqawqis the ruler of Egypt, Harith Gassani the governor of Syria, Heraclius the Roman Emperor, Armah the Negus of Aksumite Empire, Chosroes II the Khosrau of Persia. The two leaders that I'm most concerned with are Egypt and Aksumite Empires.

These letters represent a forced cultural change in the form of what amounts to get down or lay down. These letters had a criminal undertone. As the Islamic Empire expanded, Islamic culture and religion spread with it. They were forcing or manipulating their way of life in another culture.

Humans develop social-cultural systems with attitudes, beliefs, ethics, sacred places, worldviews, customs, and traditions. These concepts loosely define religion. There is no established consensus or scholarly agreement on what defines religion and how the parts go together to organize religion. Some religions (cultural systems) may or may not have Gods, goddesses, festivals, dance, art, music, meditation, funerary services, matrimonial services, prayer, veneration of ancestors, or deities that promote a people's culture and give them agency over their land. Cultural systems (Religions) promote worldviews, sacred histories, sacred texts, holy places, and symbols. The letters to the heads of cultures (Heads of states) said to be written by Muhumid attack the very fabric that makes us unique as humans, our culture. Let us look at the two letters promoting an Arab worldview on why the Egyptians and the Nagus of Ethiopia should accept the deified ancestor of the Muslims.

Letter of the Prophet Muhammed to Armah, the Negus:

"In the name of God, Most Gracious, Most Merciful.

From Muhammad the Prophet of God to Najashi, the King of Abyssinia:

"Peace to you that I thank God for you,

God, there is no god, but He, the King, the Holy Peace insured dominant, and I bear witness that Jesus son of Mary, the Spirit of God and his speech was delivered to the Virgin Mary the good bunker.

God created Jesus from his spirit, just as he created Adam with his hand, and I invite you and your soldiers to God Almighty, has reached and advised receive my advice, and peace be upon those who follow the guidance.

Seal: Muhammad, the Prophet of God." (1)

Right from the start, Muhammad attempts to sway the King away from his gods. He does this by acknowledging the parts of the Ethiopian gods that the Muslims agreed with. He then invites the King and his soldiers to his God. Muhammad promises peace to those that follow the guidance of Allah. Without having to say it, the message is clear. Follow Allah for Peace or reject Allah for war.

The following letter follows the same pattern.

"In the name of God, Most Gracious, Most Merciful.

From the Apostle of God to the Mukaukis, chief of the Copts. Peace be upon him who follows the guidance.

Next, I summon you with the appeal of creating peace:

submit your will to God, and you will have peace. God shall give you your reward twofold. But if you decline, then on you is the guilt of the Copts.

Say, "O People of the Book! Let us come to common terms: that we will worship none but Allah, associate none with Him, nor take one another as lords instead of Allah." But if they turn away, then say, "Bear witness that we have submitted `to Allah alone`."

(Quran, Chapter: Aal Imran "The House of Joachim" 3:64)

Seal: Muhammad, the Prophet of God" (2)

Arab imperialism in the form of a merciful God (deified ancestor) plays out in these letters. How arrogant does a group of people have to be for them to think that their culture is the only way? The Muslim conquest starts with disorganized pillaging raids by non-Muslim Arab tribes. These raids would extend into wars of conquest. Scholars claim that these wars had been planned military activities. Whatever the reason for the expansion and migration into other kingdoms, it unified the Arab tribes under Islam. How attractive is religion a unifying force that promoted raids, pillaging, death, destruction, and subjugation?

At this time, past accomplishments meant nothing, for Africans were ill-prepared for highly motivated, fast-moving, well-armed, well-prepared Arabs. During this time in history, Muslims had control over far-flung trade routes and critical trading networks. The Arab religion did what it was supposed to do, revolutionized ideologies and political structures of the Arabian society giving them the capability to expand and grow an empire. In some cases, African kings, chiefs, and queens converted to Islam to access trade routes. The general population was often slow to convert but would succumb later by mixing the indigenous systems with the new invading religions. This theme seems to be a recurring picture as the coming of Christianity established a foothold with the same tactics 800 years later enslave, convert, and disrupt the cultural worldview.

As African groups became absorbed into Islam, this never stopped the African genius from rising to the top. One of the great Ethiopian descended Muslim thinkers was Al-Jahiz. This Ethiopian studied and attended lectures on philology and lexicography. His appetite for learning and desire for knowledge helped him write over 200 books, of which 30 survive, and is a clear indication of his African genius. The most spectacular and important to human history (African history) is his encyclopedia with seven volumes. The Book of Animals (*Kitab al-Hayawan*), as it is formally known, is one of the first books to foreshadow evolution by way of natural selection briefly. In The Book of Animal (lV,68), Al-Jahiz says, "Lice are black on the head of a young man with black hair, light on that of a hoary old man." This statement is the beginning outline of natural selection. Al-Jahiz also explains the struggle for life by way of Natural selection in that same encyclopedia before Charles Darwin.

(3) 600 years later, Charles Darwin would propose in his book ***On the Origin of Species*** (or, more completely, ***On the Origin of Species by Means of Natural Selection, or the Preservation of Favoured Races in the Struggle for Life***) the theory of evolution. Charles Darwin would become one of the first people to admit that Africa was the homeland of all living humans. Al-Jahiz opened the door for us to understand human history in its blackness.

Bro Ankh

sources:

(1) https://en.wikipedia.org/wiki/Muhammad%27s_letters_to_the_heads_of_state

(2) Margoliouth, D. S. (1905). Mohammed and the Rise of Islam (Third Edition., p. 365). New York; London: G. P. Putnam's Sons; The Knickerbocker Press

(3) "Darwin's Ghosts, By Rebecca Stott *independent.co.uk*. Retrieved 19 June 2012.."

A 13th Century engraving of Fil on display in British Museum of Natural History

صورة الفيل

As the Islamic legend of the 'Year of the Elephant' indicates, the elephant is regarded by Muslims as creature of remarkable wisdom and is treated with due respect. A versatile beast, it is able to exist in a variety of climates and consequently has played a major part in the local and trading economy of many African peoples. Unlike the Indian elephant, it is rarely domesticated; rather it is hunted with great ritual for its meat, ivory, bristle, and hide. Even the ear has its use - as the skin of royal drums.
This miniature is from The Description of Animals, an Arab bestiary done before 1258.

Introduction

This journey began a few years ago to gain a greater understanding of answering a recent claim made by an African American brother by the name of Lord Abba. Lord Abba claimed that Islam came into West Africa in peace and spread without bloodshed. It's bothersome because African Americans have given Islam in America a pass due to the influence of the NOI and its appeal to emotional propaganda. African Americans' biggest influences are Malcolm X and Khalid Muhammad, yet both left the nation but held Islam near and dear. Before the Transatlantic kidnapping, Arabs saw fit to enslave, castrate, rape, pillage, and manipulate Africans all over. Also, when Islam is discussed in the West by blacks, its history of enslaving us becomes irrelevant because our oppression in the new world only exists due to the European nation's thirst for power and control over a people and its resources.

Before our ancestors encountered the Portuguese and other European nations, Islam traveled from afar with the influence of trade. This text sets out to answer the role of Islam and syncretism, Jihad and its use in the land of the blacks, race, and slavery, if Islam spread peacefully, and white rule in the land of the blacks.

According to Arabs scholars, Africans, and Europeans, we will use the best available data. This project contains over 20 plus sources evenly distributed to argue for or against the research questions. With all biases removed, I could now formulate an honest conclusion. Before this text became available to be read, a collective reviewed, critiqued, scrutinized, and falsified the data.

"It should be known that god has chosen certain individuals. He honored them by addressing them. He created them so that they might know Him. He made them connecting links between Himself and His servants. These individuals are to acquaint their fellow men with what is good for them and to urge them to let themselves be guided aright. They are to make it their task to keep their fellow men out of the fire of hell and to show them the path to salvation. The knowledge that god gave them and the wonders He manifested through their statements indicated that there exist things beyond the reach of man that can be learned only from god through the mediation of such individuals and that these individuals themselves cannot know unless god instructs them. Muhammad said: 'Indeed, I know only what God taught me.' It should be known that the information they give is intrinsically and necessarily true, as will become clear when the reality of prophecy is explained." - (Rosenthal, Dawood, Lawrence 2005:70)

Was this Islam's intention when it revealed itself to Africa in the early dawn of the day as it traveled through the North into Mauritania and down into the belly of Bilad al-Sudan? It peacefully came to save the lives of individuals who were bound for the gates of hell who knew no way or the existence of a creator who summoned someone from afar to spare their lives of these individuals from evil. This messenger, a unique being named Muhammad, seems to understand around him the unconsciousness of his people, and he once said when asked about how 'god' came to him his response: 'We shall lay upon you a weighty message.' (Rosenthal, Dawood, Lawrence 2005:70)

So, the fate of Africans and a hereafter reside in a man they would never know or meet. I find this calling from god unique but not personal because, in history, we tend to hear this from preachers when they tell their stories about how they came to stand before their congregations. Could it be said that god only speaks to those he ordains to be prophets, and in the case of Prophet Muhammad, he states: 'Every Prophet was given signs likely to provide reassurance for humanity. What I have been given is a revelation that was revealed to me. Therefore, I hope to have the greatest number of followers on the day of resurrection.' (Rosenthal, Dawood, Lawrence 2005:73-74) As stated early, we will deal with one claim and a few questions in this work, and if the Prophet shall serve himself right on the day of resurrection, Islam spread in peace and saved the souls of those in Bilad al-Sudan.

'Had you given away all the riches of the earth, you could not have so united them. But god has united them.' Qur'an 8:63

Chapter One - My Hypothesis

Within the confines of my research questions, I set out to answer questions related to Lord Abbas claim which put my research into proper perspective. When did Islam enter Bilad al-Sudan, and who brought it with them? Was it peaceful or by force? What Role Did Syncretism Play in Bilad al-Sudan? What is the meaning of Jihad & and its use in Bilad al-Sudan? What role did race and slavery play? All of these questions needed answering for me because I was stuck wondering why Lord Abba would make his initial assertion that Islam came in peace.

As stated in my introduction, I started this journey a few years ago due to a claim made by Lord Abba. One evening, he was broadcasting on his YouTube channel responding to Mossi Warrior Clan Affiliate Class of Shabazz. Due to the back and forth between the two regarding misinformation cited on the Livestream by Lord Abba, Shabazz attempted to address the errors and points of contention that were incorrect. In that exchange, he stated that Islam came in peace, and I took exception with that based on principal sources I had read, but to adequately address that claim, I needed to remove all biases and tackle that question head-on.

Before opening the last ten books I've read, I wrote my hypothesis down based on incomplete data for a reason. Scholarship directs you to do so within the confines of methodology, showing my errors, flaws, and all. I never took an interest in learning anything about Islam and Arabs because both have preyed on Africa since they stepped foot along the Nile around 630 AD. The spread of Islam dripped in the blood of Africans from all directions as conversion forced the people's will to either die or accept it. The interest of Arabs focus was on Africa's natural resources, and that influence led to greed which would redirect the history of those who encountered Islam.

Jihad had to mean force because it seems to give credence to the wrath Islam bestowed on Africans, especially in Bilad al-Sudan. What other reason would traditionalists have to rid themselves of their cultural identity and accept the ways of an Arab? Syncretism would allow Muslims to rewrite history in West Africa, forcing traditionalists to lose faith in their worldview while entrusting a foreign perspective. I mean, without the Sharia (law), Arabs must've used force because Africans couldn't have known anything about a prophet, their religion, or its purpose. Which meant those in Bilad al-Sudan and many other parts of Africa were at a complete disadvantage, and whatever beliefs and understandings that existed suddenly became non-existent. Based on a lack of unknowing, unfamiliarity, language barriers, and worldview, Arabs had to come by force and sword in the name of Allah and forcibly convert.

Slavery became synonymous with race because of the ideological views Arabs had toward non-Arabs. They saw themselves as a force to be reckoned with, and you see this in their literature and the way they write about themselves throughout history. My working hypothesis began to take shape based on evident research between cross-referencing sources and extensive research that transpired before writing this book. In no way should this be taken as a conclusion.

One should look at this the same way one would at a trial, and I am making my opening argument based on my educated guess. As we set forth to answer each question, we will go in the direction the evidence takes us and conclude based on the collections of facts. Still, I want the reader to recall my initial hypothesis because it is a starting point that some stop and argue from ignorance.

Chapter Two
The Coming of Islam & The Role of Syncretism

The First Revelation

"In the name of Allah, the Beneficent, the Merciful. In the name of of they Lord who, createth man from a clot. And thy Lord is the Most Bounteous, Who teachers by the pen, teacheth man that which he knew not. Nay, but verily man is rebellious that he thinkers himself independent! Lo! Unto thy Lord is the return. Hast thou seen him who dissuadeth a slave when he prayeth? Hast thou seen if he [relieth] on guidance [of Allah] or enjoineth peity? Hast thou seen if he denieth [Allah's guidance] and is forward? Is he then unaware that Allah seeth? Nay, but if he cease not. We will seize him by the forelock - the lying, sinful forelock - then let him call upon his henchmen! We will call the guards of hell. Nay! Obey not thou him. But prostrate thyself, and draw near [unto Allah]."
Prophet Muhammad

Historians argue that the spread of Islam began when Muhammad claimed to receive his divine word from the archangel Gabriel what many believe to be his revelation. Theology states that only the real prophets can receive the word from the higher spirits; no evidence substantiates the claim, but his followers will receive it; however, Islam grew more following his death. "After the death of Prophet Muhammad in 632 AD, Arab Muslims forces overtook most elements of the Byzantine-ruled areas of the Middle East, A.D. then moved into the African continent, took over Egypt from Byzantines, and then moving westwards along North Africa. They reached what is now Tunisia and established their fortress-town at Qayrawān in 670, and by the end of the seventh century, they had occupied the land up to the coast of the Atlantic Ocean, though not taken over territory very far south of the Mediterranean Sea." (Hunwick 2010:25) Hunwick called North Africa the foreigner's quarter because foreigners mainly inhabited it. (Hunwick 1972:117) That had to inspire the coming of Islam in Bilad al-Sudan and West Africans first glimpse of its influence. Before that, no remanence of Islam existed in the land of the blacks.

Many would assume that due to North African' conquest,' Islam would enter West Africa similarly; however, that would not be the case earlier. During the settlement of Muslims in the Maghreb, certain Berbers began to be influenced by traders during caravans who made successful trips back and forth across North Africa. "The first of the Saharan Berbers whose conversion is attested seem to have been the Lamtūna, who is said to have accepted Islam in the second decade of the eighth century, followed shortly afterward by the Massūfa and Djuddāla. Their Islam, however, must have been only a thin veneer for many centuries to come; the whole history of the beginning of the Almoravid movement furnishes eloquent evidence of the superficial Islamization month these three Berber peoples." (Hrbek, Fasi1992:38)

According to more modern scholarship, Islam entered West Africa 7 years prior. Modern scholarship states that a specific Berber tribe who lived in Ghana had been converted to Islam by some people who had come into close contact with the Ibadi around the 9th century who professed to be doing missionary work in the name of Islam. "It is now quite clear that Ibādi traders penetrated the Sudan much earlier than orthodox Sunnites, and it is likely that some of the first converts among the Sudanese were won for Islam precisely by proselytizing efforts of the Ibādites." (Hrbek, Fasi1992:38) We can concede here that the influence of Islam on West Africans began with Islamic missionaries, converted by Berbers of numerous tribes, and merchant traders controlling commerce.

However, "Restrictions were certainly maintained in this first contact situation upon where the Muslim merchants could travel (Devisse 1992:204), and this would not have relaxed until conversion to Islam had spread beyond mercantile and perhaps nomad contexts. We have references in the Arabic historical sources which imply that West Africans restricted the movement of Arab and Berber merchants. Yaqut (d. 1229), in describing the inhabitants of their manners, are reported through those people never allow a merchant to see them. (Levtzion and Hopkins 1981:170). But certainly, by the time Ibn Battuta visited the western Sahel in the mid-fourteenth century, intercourse between foreign merchants and the indigenous population was common, and no restrictions appear to have been placed upon his travels (Hamdun and King 1994)." (Insoll 2003:222)

So, the actual order of business with the Berbers and Muslims in West Africa led to restrictions initially. We know of this based on previous conditions that had been in place prior but eased once integration began. Under certain conditions, this would allow, of course, an opportunity for the spread of Islam to spread among the people. We will discuss conversion in a future chapter to clear up any confusion; however, we now have a summarized view of how the spread of Islam and its presence surfaced in West Africa, and syncretism would take center stage.

"While initially, all the inhabitants of West Africa practiced their indigenous religions, since the tenth century A.D. Silam, which was brought across the desert, has gained many converts in the Savannah. In more recent times, it has gained converts in the forest belt too." (Crowder 1977:6). With the spread of Islam, Religious syncretism became inevitable for Chieftains and Kings to participate in trade. The Muslim conversion took place with heads of states converting to Islam slowly but surely. Anyone could expect this to happen. "Al-Bakrī reports that when a new ruler was installed at Gao, he was given a sword, a shield and a copy of the Quran, which were said to have been sent from the Caliph as his insignia of office." (Hrbek, Fasi1992:40)

One of the early chiefdoms of the Malinke converted along with the Mais of Kanem, Hummay Djilmi, and many others. The conversions by prominent leadership meant that Islam would be readily accepted.

"African rulers in general accepted fairly readily a division of space and labor which ensured that the administrators they required would be available to them in the towns which had been wholly or partly Islamized, while the rural world constituted an inexhaustible source of compliant agricultural manpower whose conversion was not a matter of urgency. Being content with the conversion of the princes who, in the long term, were the guarantors of the conversion of the masses, Islam probably adopted a 'pastoral' attitude which was also to be found in Christian Europe at the same periods." (Dramani-Issifou 1992:52)

Also, what made Islam appealing was that it became popularized; however, this was not the case earlier on, Islam remained in pockets of West Africa where trade routes existed, and traditionalists would venture further into the bush in some instances to avoid coming into contact with it. What changed over time was that Islam preached unity and a pact among humankind, but most importantly, its acceptance of certain African traditions and customs aligned itself with traditional beliefs.

"The spread of Islam as an institutionalized system of beliefs and practices or as a way of life was not, therefore, only neutralized by the traditional African perception of religion, but where Islam was adopted it meant a blending with, rather than a complete break away from, indigenous practices. Consequently, African Muslim and Christian groups and individuals throughout the continent continue, after centuries of conversion, to combine their traditional cultural and religious customs with Arab-Islamic and Western-Christian ones." (Azumah 2020:51)

Amulets have always been a big part of African traditions, and Islam provided similar understanding and protection. "Owusu-Ansah asserts that Islam was put to many uses in Asante. These uses included amulets for war medicine and cures for bed-wetting, smallpox, impotence, infertility, leprosy, and ulcers, to name but a few. This demonstrates the African deployment of religious symbolism to generate spiritual power. In this case, foreign missionary religions were co-opted by indigenous religious practice." (Curry 2006:154)

Also, it was a part of Muslim culture that made it attractive to add the thoughts of multiple wives mirrored the ideology of West Africans. In short, Islam would mask traditions in certain areas, given the people something they could relate to and not have to abandon.

"A key recurring feature of Islam in sub-Saharan Africa is the notion of continuity, how the pre-Islamic foundations and religious heritage have been incorporated in a syncretic process, a process defined as 'basic not only to religious and ritual but to the 'predicament of culture' in general' (Shaw and Stewart 1994:1). As well as syncretism, the coexistence of traditional beliefs might exist, with a literal separation perhaps employed with Islam defined as a religion. However, traditional beliefs and practices as custom, as seen among the Berti of the Nilotic Sudan (Holy 1991), or as evident archaeologically in the inland Niger delta area of Mali - as attested by the growth in terracotta figurine production (R.J. McIntosh 1998), or the persistence of urn burial (Bedaux 1979) - after conversion to Islam had begun in parts of the region.

African traditional religions frequently appear to have meshed with Islam rather than acting as agents of confrontation with it. The history and archaeology of Africa show that various traditions and faiths could coexist. Today, however, there are many tensions precisely along these lines. Nations created by colonial powers - the Nilotic Sudan, for instance (Beswick and Spaulding 2000) - are now embroiled precisely in religious and other ethnic conflicts." (Insoll 2003:400)

Malian Sonni Ali could define the best example of this syncretism. Griots state that he would often go to the bush in times of need where he would practice his traditional beliefs and prepare himself for war, but upon his return, he held the views of Islam just as near and dear. "The situation of Islam under Sunni Ali in Songhai, then, was that of a balance of forces between it and the indigenous religion. At the same time strong currents of Islamic influence were being felt in the surrounding territories and in Timbuktu the learned men were already beginning to become a force of Muslim opposition to royal practices adjudged to be un-Islamic." (Hunwick 1927:122)

Although some Arabs saw this as a detriment, others would take offense to this practice and would claim he is playing a Muslim to earn his piece and presence. "Though some West African rulers transmitted and embodied aspects of Islam, others did not embrace Islam because it threatened dimensions of their indigenous religions and polity. For example, Sonni Ali, in 1465 in the Songhay empire, purged some aspects of Islam and borrowed others to combine them with pre-Islamic practices for his political gains. People like Sonni Ali are known as Mukhallitwn because they combine Islam with traditional faith. When Islam gained some roots among the ruling classes, the new underpinnings of their rule to Islam, this practice, according to Sanneh, produced important environmental flexibility for the appropriation of Islam. However, such hybridized Islam was disapproved of by orthodox Muslims who sought to 'Arabize' the Africans. Sonni Ali and others like him demonstrated a political astute and selective use of Islam. On the other hand, the Askia Muhammad Toure who desposed Sonni Ali embraced a zealous Islam and repudiated the hybridized Islam of his predecessor." (Curry 2006:151-52) Another account on Sonni Ali and his inability to conform to Islam states, "Ali had no use for Islam, the religion of urban communities. Its learned men constituted a state and were critical of rulers for lukewarmness in Islam and indulgence in pagan rites. Confident in his own power, 'Ali did not need their support and refused to compromise with a religion which involved paying allegiance to a law higher than himself." (Saad 1983:42) Sunni Ali met his demise at the hands of Askia Muhammad, who vowed to rid the old traditions and promote Islam; one might ask because he wanted to Arabize Africans to gain him certain access and prestige among the Arabs. "Askia Muhammad made considerable efforts to achieve political and social integration in line with the ethic of the Quran. To legitimize his coup d'erat, he resorted to every means afforded by the Muslim religion. He made the pilgrimage to Mecca and the title of caliph (khalifa) invested him with spiritual authority in the Sudan. In the interior, he sought the advice almost exclusively of Muslim scholars of Timbuktu and in addition requested consultation form three jurists: Abdullāh al-Ansammānī of Takedda, al-Suyūtī, and al-Maghailī." (Drammi-Issifou 1992:59)

Among the Nigerians and its famous Chronicle written about the Hausa, more specifically, "The Kano Chronicle as cited, points to the influence of Nigerian local religion on Islam. The Chronicle states that Muslim rulers of Kano consulted the Tchunburburae cult at Gagua between 1063 and 1410. Before the rulers waged war, they consulted the oracle. When Islam entered the societies in the interior of Sierra Leone, then Muslim cleric, according to Sanneh, was incorporated into 'Poor hierarchy and given a role which suited his familiarity with the sacred Arabic script. The cleric, using his knowledge (ilim awful) of the science of magic squares, which is the basis of Islamic talismans, was able to give the Poro medicine power against malevolent spirits and enemies. Other examples of mixing Islam with traditional faith exist especially at the courts of chiefs and kings in northern Ghana and in Asanteland. In Kito in northern Ghana, as Levtzion points out, is a shrine, kagbir, where the shrine-priest Kagbir-Wura: prays twice a day (mourning and evening) and fasts three days during Ramadan. He has a rosary, a Koran, and a bundle of Arabic manuscripts. He himself cannot read even an Arabic letter." (Curry 2006:153)

The thrill of having the power to manifest and control spirits or utilize magic against its enemies was an appealing narrative that numerous West African chiefs and kings held in high regard as they looked for advantages to expand their empires and control trade. "In pre-colonial Middle Volta Basin in the Gold Coast (Ghana), according to Levtzion, there were times when Muslim clerics gave up their practice as Muslims and served as diviners in local cults." (Curry 2006:153) The practice of Islam was as common as a light switch in a dark room easily accessible when needed, but when it served no purpose, it became less beneficial.

In conclusion: syncretism began to expand throughout West Africa while comparing spirits and professing deities to have the exact likeness "Islam has achieved the double victory of successful conversion and generosity towards African value [is] a contradictory state of affairs that discredits that procedure. The imputing to Islam of a wide degree of flexibility in its interaction with African societies completes the process by robbing traditional societies of a crucial element of their heritage; [namely] the tradition of 'enclavement' (which accords protection and guarantee to stranger and non-kin groups) on the one hand, and on the other the inclusive and tenacious nature of local religions." (Azumah 2020:34-35) Certain circumstances would shed light on cultural practices that didn't meet the need of the people. That favored Islam over traditional customs that quickly changed how West Africans saw the old belief systems. Later, the detachment of shrines all over West Africa started to become defaced, destroyed, and forgotten about if they did not serve its people well when needed.

"Facing a national calamity of drought in Malal, the ruler sought help from the indigenous religious specialists, but the drought persisted. It was only when a visiting Muslim cleric prescribed prayers to be performed that rains fell to end the drought. This dramatic relief led the ruler to accept Islam and demolish the local palace shrines. The ruler deployed his political power to end an indigenous religion and to embrace Islam, because of the need Islam met at the time." (Curry 2006:154-55)

Chapter Three
The Meaning of Jihad & It's Use in Bilad al-Sudan

Hadith 14

عَنْ ابْنِ مَسْعُودٍ رَضِيَ اللهُ عَنْهُ قَالَ: قَالَ رَسُولُ اللَّهِ صلى الله عليه و سلم

"لَا يَحِلُّ دَمُ امْرِئٍ مُسْلِمٍ [يشهد أن لا إله إلا الله، وأني رسول الله] إِلَّا بِإِحْدَى ثَلَاثٍ: الثَّيِّبُ الزَّانِي، وَالنَّفْسُ بِالنَّفْسِ، وَالتَّارِكُ لِدِينِهِ الْمُفَارِقُ لِلْجَمَاعَةِ".

، [رَوَاهُ الْبُخَارِيُّ]

On the authority of Abdullah Ibn Masud (may Allah be pleased with him) who said: The Messenger of Allah (peace be upon him) said:

"It is not permissible to spill the blood of a Muslim except in three [instances]: the married person who commits adultery, a life for a life, and the one who forsakes his religion and separates from the community."

[Al-Bukhari & Muslim]

Jihad could be seen as synonymous with slavery because the act of Jihad had rules; those rules involved the legality of enslaving people, and the acceptance of slavery is justified according to Muslim law (Sharia). Also, Jihad meant forced conversion; this is seen throughout its implementation across the Continent of Africa. With Jihad telling to exert or make a determined effort, one would conclude that Muslim intention was to force its beliefs upon those they saw as 'pagans' and nonbelievers of what the Prophet preached. Remember, "Islam is the eternal world religion which came into existence for the happiness of humankind, and to guide it to what is best for it in this world and the next. It is not possible for any system of law, whether religious or civil, to produce that which was produced by the scripture of Islam, the Noble Quran since it is a revelation from the Knowing One, the Wise One. Nothing is hidden from Him, and His ordinances are not inspired by them which is not in accord with the interests of humanity as a whole." (Hunwick & Powell 2010:17)

To understand Islam, one must remember sharia 'law' prohibits exerting one's efforts to spread its Prophet's word and the religion.

Jihad simply means in English to exert efforts, but some would say it means to strive or make a determined effort. In an article written by Robert Rabil in the Washington Institute, he states, 'In Arabic, the word 'jihad' broadly means 'to strive' or make a 'determined effort,' and a Mujahid is someone who strives or strives engages in Jihad. Jihad is often expanded to the term jihad fi sable Allah (Jihad I the path of god) to distinguish the term from pre-Islamic usage and assert that the 'determined effort' is carried out according to god's divine mandate. However, the specifically religious connotations of the word have different shades of meaning even in the Koran, where the connotation of jihad shifts along with the changing sociopolitical environments under which Prophet Muhammad developed Islam.' (Rabil 2018)

Azumuah argues: "The definition of Jihad has become something of an enigma since the beginning of the twentieth century due to various factors. These include the fact that the term 'jihad' has a rather wide range of meanings and lends itself to differing interpretations and emphasis. Second, Muslim sources such as the Quran and sunna are themselves not immediately clear on the subject. Third, early and modem intra/anti-Muslim polemics and apologetics have added to the enigma. Jihad is the Arabic verbal noun derived from the verb jahada, which means 'strain,' 'exertion,' 'endeavor,' etc., on behalf or for the sake of something. Jihad is translated by E.W. Lane as 'the using, or exerting one's utmost power, efforts, endeavors, or ability, in contending with an object of disapprobation … namely a visible enemy, the devil, and oneself'. Lane goes on to point out that Jihad came to be used by Muslims to signify fighting or waging war against 'unbelievers and the like' as a religious duty." (Azumah 2020:64-65)

To be honest, many Muslim apologists try to hide the fact that forced conversion was a reality that helped it spread. Due to romanticism, this conflict of interest diminished the role of indigenous culture in Bilad al-Sudan. "Quranic stipulations on the subject itself range from verses that enjoin Muslims to be tolerant towards non-Muslims to those that permit Muslims to fight and slay 'unbelievers' who persecute them, to verses that instruct Muslims to make war upon non-Muslims 'wherever ye find them' until or unless 'they repent and establish worship and pay the poor dues,' in what has come to be known as the 'sword verse.'" (Azumah 2020:65)

"The imam (the Muslim ruler conducting the jihad) should look into the fate of adult male prisoners and take whichever of the following options he considers most beneficial: to put them to death, to release them without penalty, to ask ransom for them, to demand capitation tax (jizya), or to enslave them." (Hunwick & Powell 2010:23) Overall the justifications for exerting themselves by force, trickery, or otherwise established the evolution of Jihad in Bilad al-Sudan. Jihad also fed the slave trade, which brought in prominent prophets for Muslim rulers, which would play a massive role in the Trans-Atlantic slave trade. "For many centuries, the commonest way West Africans to end up in the Arab world, especially in the Arab states in North Africa, was through slavery. Arabs were holding Africans as enslaved people in Arabia even before the beginning of the religion of Islam, though such Africans had come from the area of what is now Ethiopia. When Islam became the fundamental religion of Arabs, it became lawful only for people considered to be 'pagans' to be held by Arabs as enslaved people." (Hunwick 2010:63) From Islam's earliest onset, it seems to be used as a tool to enslave and conquer those foreign to the ideological and cultural perspectives of the Arab world. As the spread of Islam commences, enslavement is pursued. According to the Quran, slavery is justified, "Prior to the nineteenth century, there is no evidence of condemnation of slavery by Muslim writers, nor any attempt to justify the institution. Enslavement was considered retribution for the rejection of the Islamic faith since the sole legal method of obtaining an enslaved person (at least in theory) was through the defeat of non-Muslims in a jihād that had as its aim to 'make the word of God supreme and to bring men to His religion which he chose for His servants.' In the nineteenth and twentieth centuries, some Muslim writers felt a need to rationalize the acceptance of slavery in Islamic thinking, in response to European condemnation of slavery and criticism of Islam." (Hunwick & Powell 2009:13)

In the Muqaddimah Ibn Khaldûn states, 'In the Muslim community, the holy war is a religious duty, because of the universalism of the Muslim mission and (the obligation to) convert everybody to Islam either by persuasion or by force. Therefore, caliphate and royal authority are united in Islam, so that the person in charge can devote the available strength to both of them at the same time." Khaldûn continued to state that other religious sects did not have this universal mission; therefore, 'holy war' was not a part of who they were or what they stood for, which provided prestige among the Muslims as they seemed to justify the forced conversions and control over a people who were ignorant of their intentions. To be honest, Muslims were not about mixing cultures; they intended to impose their will on the rest of the world in the name of Allah.

"Indeed, Islam does not accept that people should have customs or traditions other than religious ones; for if Allah's way is a comprehensive way of life, what is there for custom and tradition? S.S. Nyang writes approvingly about the 'two processes of de-traditionalization and Islamization' during the jihad campaigns where 'successes of Muslims in many areas of the West Sudan led to gradual destruction of the traditional cults and emasculation of the old aristocracy." (Azumah 2020:8)

So, gradually the use of Jihad in Bilad al-Sudan meant to impose its will physically or psychologically as well as to spread its religion and domination among those who did not adhere to or subscribe to Islamic thought culturally. "The eighteenth and nineteenth-century jihad movements and the policies and attitudes of the jihadists towards traditional believers and indigenous African elements belie claims that Islam, or rather 'orthodox' Islam, is 'generous' towards old Africa. For the jihadists' programs of Islamization have hitherto been depicted by key Western observers and the overwhelming majority of African Muslims as the nearest African Muslims ever came to expressing 'orthodox Islam.' And these jihadist policies of Islamization, as pointed out by H.J. Fisher, sometimes involved sharp and even cruel insistence upon proper standards, and an equally sharp break with local traditions. No one who has read of the stern law-enforcement of the theocracies - or, the eye-witness accounts of fatal floggings in Bornu, for violations of Ramadan, early in the nineteenth century - will ever think of that kind of Islam as colored no more than water. It was dyed with blood." (Azumah 2020:9) The blood that is on the hands of Islam has been glossed over and swept under the rug because of what exactly has yet to be determined unless it's being sold an afterlife, virgins, or being in the good graces of a deity that is foreign to you.

"The adoption of Islam, the religion of the foreign traders, most of who were also proselytizers, in the 11th century A.D., helped in accelerating socio-political and cultural developments. Expeditions were jihads against non-Muslims or razzias against enemies of the state." (Ajayi & Uya 2010:50) Jihad served serval purposes: gathering enslaved people and establishing a holy presence among those who accepted Islam and converted. It was also a political tool one could immediately witness based on the climate of trade and enslaved people and ideology that traveled from place to place. "To make it more difficult was the fact that the emerging emirates were based on a new religion, Islam. This meant not only an effort to build mega political systems where none existed but also based on a new religion. This was unlike the Hausa states which were largely Islamic with only backsliding rulers. Once the jihadists supplanted those rulers, the ferocity of the conflicts subsided. In short, in our area of study conflicts and the capture of slaves continued in most of the area until the inception of the colonial period." (Ajayi & Uya 2010:51) It also helped establish dominance among trade routes and a presence in those market areas that would allow them to tax people and continue the introduction of Islam to non-converts. Jihad then became a staple of Islam used to convert people in Bilad al-Sudan as this tool was essential in the expansion of this foreign religion.

"Hiskett, in following a tradition set by the H.F.C. Smith and Murray last in the 1960s, writes about and presents the jihad tradition as 'reform movements' aimed at bringing about the proper observances of Islam. No attempt whatsoever is made to give a detached analysis of the jihad movement, which many well-meaning Muslims at the time opposed and condemned. Indeed, Hiskett's Sword of Truth could not have been better written by Dan Fodio himself. Hiskett joins the jihadists in calling those Muslims who opposed it 'venal' or 'corrupt' scholars, and, as the title of his book indicates, regarded the jihadists' story as the 'truth.' What we have in the Sword of Truth, in effect, is not even the Muslim view, but a factional, albeit triumphant, Muslim view. The views of Muslims and non-Muslims who challenged the 'truth' of the jihadists and suffered the pain of the sword are simply ignored." (Azumah 2022:11) The non-pagan view is not considered when it comes to the utilization of Jihad and the brutal objective of the people who saw it as a despicable way to approach conversion. Let me be clear the people who professed issues with Jihad were already converted themselves and opposed the blood bath it left.

"Another major jihad after that of Dan Fodio was the Jihad of al-Hajj 'Umar Tal (d. 1864), a Tubular of Futa Toro in the Senegambian region. Another jihad of the period worth mentioning was that initiated by Samori Ture. Samori's Jihad is of particular interest, in that, unlike most of the other main jihadists, he was of the Mande and not Fulbe tribe. (Azumah 2020:78-79) A fair share of jihadist movements was initiated by certain sects such as the Fulbe and Tukulor; these reoccurrences happened so much that these movements became to be seen as racial, classist, and political. Leaders of the jihadist movements, according to tradition, are seen as champions or moguls among their people due to this romanced ideological perspective. "Jihad is to be strictly limited to the fighting of infidels ... It is the tyrant Muslims who are to be fought I order that the Sharia become established ... And, such fighting cannot be recognized as Jihad. And the person who dies participating in such activity will not receive the honors of a martyr in Jihad." (Azumah 2020:87) Azumah continues to make a good point that if the Jihadists were seen as reformers, their actions do not qualify to be called jihads.

Jihadists' view must be considered, especially from a political perspective toward traditionalists, because the opportunity to be seen in the eyes of Islam as a servant of Allah and continuing the work of the Prophet was essential and respected among Muslims. Justified or not, jihads were about domination, control, and the spread of Islam. Ultimately people set out to please the Prophet; dead or alive, it was reverence being paid.

"Unbelievers are to be fought, killed and their property, children and women seized as booty." - Dan Fodio

According to Muslims, to jihadists, traditionalists did not deserve to rule and had no right to establish any type of dominance over commerce, land, and or people. They also believed that nonbelievers could not rule over believers. This direct conflict was just enough to wage Jihad on every single traditionalist believer to encounter and convert as many people as possible. Muslims dictated who owned what and how much of that was determined by their religious status among its people.

"So in their twin mission of 'de-traditionalization and Islamization,' the jihadists made the old aristocracies their chief targets and, in effect, demanded immediate and unconditional cultural, political and socio-religious surrender." (Azumah 2020:97) To be honest, traditionalists were seen as low-class citizens in their land and reduced to such instantly in the eyes of Islam. Sharia justified this ideology, and it was enforced, which promoted de-Africanizing whoever they encountered.

"The Fulani jihads could be described in their aims as 'anti-syncretic,' as described by Shaw and Stewart (1994:7). Yet the notion of anti-syncretic, if we are to use this as a definition for the ethos underpinning the jihads, must also be considered, for it is not value-free. It, too, is a construct with its associated claims of 'authenticity and 'purity. It frequently acts, as Shaw and Stewart (1994:12) also note, as a 'dominate reading in discourse of nationalist, ethnic or regional identity. Essentially, the Fulani jihads might equate with what Eaton (1993) would define as a case of 'displacement,' yet they too served a purpose wider than merely eradicating what was perceived as lax Islam and practices integrated; from traditional religions." (Insoll 2003:302)

In conclusion, Jihad meant to exert or the exertion of which clearly was understood as a force to spread and conquer in the name of 'Allah' from one tribe or clan to another. This meant conversion by bloodshed or political gain. Jihad was applauded among the Muslim world as if 'The Prophet' would have been proud of how non-Muslims had converted and expanded their belief system.

Jihad was a dangerous tool used to manipulate the weak and murder the strong. It was about the advancement of Muslim rule and nonbelievers who were enslaved and could be given a choice to convert to spare themselves with no idea of what the new future would be held.

Traditionalists stood no chance as they did earlier on during the coming of Islam, and Jihad would be an enforcer among those who avoided conversion. One could conclude that to rule or have access to some form of control in your area; you had to have at least committed one Jihad to be taken seriously among one's peers.

Adopting a foreign religion could never be a good thing for West Africans, especially in the coming centuries with the loss of history, culture, and tradition. Jihad brought the acceptance of foreign and the belittling of an old guard. The ancestors became irrelevant while Allah was the focal point. Those who refused had to run and seek cover in the bush, while others accepted a blend of Islam that would only last until a new guard ushered in changes. Without Jihad, Islam would have been rejected and not have penetrated West Africa in its early inception. Islam was put on a pedestal and sold to the people as a cure-all and the real key to a prosperous afterlife. While Muslim presence dominated trade routes and political prowess, conversion by the sword was a staple used to continue the spread of Islam. Today we can see the results of the jihadist movements when we look at different West African countries with a predominantly Muslim presence with numerous converts unfamiliar with their traditional ways of old.

Chapter Four
The Role Race & Slavery Played Among The Muslim World

"The mobilization of local ideas about racial difference has been important in generating - and intensifying - civil wars that have occurred since the end of colonial rule in all of the countries that straddle the southern edge of the Sahara Desert. From Sudan to Mauritania, the racial categories deployed in contemporary conflicts often hearken back to an older history in which blackness could be equated with slavery and non blackness with predatory and uncivilized banditry." - Bruce Hall

Worldview shapes the mindset, and we see this in early Arab African interactions. Before Arabs reached the Western part of Africa, according to them, in their own words, they had already classified Africans as inferior people based on the color of their skin, which emphasized a negative representation culturally and religiously. With the spread of Islam on the rise for Arabs, it meant conversion at all costs. Cultural differences and skin references influenced the ideology of ignorance that would soon project itself on those in Bilād al-Sūdān. Culturally, race was used by Arabs distinctively to create a class that would denote a particular people worthy of enslavement potentially. I say potentially because not everyone was afforded the ability to gain its freedom as Bilāl b. Rabah did earlier on. Religiously Arabs saw blacks as lesser people due to the Biblical narrative and famously known 'Curse of Ham' story, but Arab scholars went so far as to create equatorial zones to help them establish their distinctions between different African tribes. To create a narrative of justification, the racial differences began to be utilized by foreigners who drew upon these distinctions. We can look at the accounts of Ībn Battūta, who is known in the Muslim world as a world-renowned traveler. Battūta colorized his encounters and distinguished people by skin tone and not based on cultural perspectives, which he and other Moroccans had been familiar with. He even talked about how blacks were only valuable as enslaved people, so when he returned from his travels elsewhere and entered the land of the blacks and witnessed them practicing Islam and ruling their lands, he was immediately not pleased with what he saw.

When I mentioned the account of Battūta, I was referring to his first and second visits to Bilād al-Sūdān. In those accounts, he equated blacks with enslaved people. However, let's review another version and how he made his distinctions based on his travels in Bilād al-Sūdān. "When the medieval Moroccan traveler Ibn Battūta (d. 1368) visited the West African Sahel in 1352 and 1353, he brought with him a North African conception of racial difference that appears to have been unfamiliar to the people with whom he interacted. In the written narrative of his travels, Ibn Battuta repeatedly distinguished between three principal types of people found in the area: Berbers, blacks, and whites. Clearly, those he identified as whites included only people like himself: Arab expatriates from North Africa or the Middle East who resided in the commercial towns along the Sahel, most of whom were merchants. With one exception, color terminology was not used to identify or describe the Berber-speaking people from the Sahel who are mentioned in his narratives, such as the Massūfa or Walata and Timbuktu or the Bardāma and Hakkār of the southern and central Sahara. For Ibn Battūta, the use of the term 'whites' implied a set of Arab Muslim cultural practices that his local Berber-speaking hosts, although Muslims, did not share. He was so scandalized by the freedom Massūfa Berber women appeared to enjoy in their social interactions with men and by their matrilineal system of descent that he compared local Berber speakers to non-Muslims he had encountered in South Asia." (Hall 2011:34-35) According to Hall, Battūta is making his distinctions based on culture and color. This allowed him to mentally create a classist mindset that would further influence other Arabic scholars who relied on his travels in other works written about West Africans, but this was the thought process of many Moroccans even to this day. Distinctions create classes, and out of those classes, Arabs equated dark skin with slavery which also was justified by the biblical narrative regarding the 'Curse of Ham.' "Arab writers inherited two principal ideas about race from pre-Islamic Mediterranean sources: an environmental theory about human differences and the biblical stories about Noah's sons Shem, Japheth, and Ham." (Hall 2011:45) Muslims were already familiar with sudanic 'Blacks' due to early trade in East Africa along the red sea. It's described by Arab writers earlier on who divided up the equatorial zones into six areas that, "The equatorial region is inhabited by communities of Blacks who are to be numbered among the savages and beasts. Their complexions and hair are burnt, and they are physically and morally deviant. Their brains almost boil from the sun's excessive heat… The human being who dwells there is a crude fellow, with a very black complexion, burnt hair, unruly, with stinking sweat, and an abnormal constitution, most closely resembling in his moral qualities a savage, or animals. He cannot dwell in the 2nd zone, let alone the 3rd and 4th, just as the people in the 1st zone live not in the 6th, nor those of the 6th in the 1st, or the equatorial region, because of the difference in the quality of the air and the heat of the sun. God knows best!" (Hunwich & Powell 2009:35)

This Understanding of equatorial zones set the Arabic worldview, immediately associating black with enslaved people. To Arabs, according to Hunwick: "were the earliest type of enslaved person known to Arabs and were the latest imported into the Arab-Islamic Middle East. One of the first black Africans known to have been in slavery in the Arabian peninsula, and to have become one of the first to have converted to Islam, was the Abyssinian called Bilāl [b. Rabah], who was owned and then freed by

Abū Bakr, the Prophet Muhammad's father-in-law and later successor (caliph), to whom he gave his freed slave, who then accepted the Prophet's message ask was given the position of muezzin -'caller to prayer' by Muhammad. Soon afterward, North Africa was occupied by Arab Muslim armies in the late seventh century, and black Africans were traded over the Sahara, and bought by Arab merchants as enslaved people - a practice which continued down to the early twentieth century." (Hunwick 2010:75)

We need to properly understand how 'The Hamitic Theory' had been utilized in Africa to proceed forward. "The Hamitic theory, which served to explain the evolution of African cultures in ancient times, has been widely used as an interpretative framework: the Hamites were, according to this theory, and African people distinct from the other blacks racially and linguistically. Among the Hamites, it included the inhabitants of the

Sahara, the Berbers, the Tubu, and the Fulani. The Hamitic theory draws a sharp distinction between the pastoral Hamites and the agricultural blacks, considering them as two separate and well-defined categories. The Hamites are regarded as having been responsible for all the progress and innovations made in Africa. That being so, the occupation of pastoral cattle-breeders is credited with cultural superiority. It is said that these white nomads have transmitted the elements of 'civilization' to the sedentary blacks." (Medeiros 1992:63) From its onset, this ideological thought process shaped the narrative of Arabs and how they viewed the Bible and used it as a tool to project its prejudices upon people that were phenotypically different from them.

"From the beginning, external sources associated bilād al-sūdān with slaving in an entirely unremarkable manner, well established by the third/ninth century given the discussion of the Fezzan. Kanem would soon develop a reputation as not only a supplier of enslaved people but as a specializing in 'black' eunuchs. The area's activities must have been considered by the eighth/fourteenth century when Ibn Battūta identified Bornu as the source of 'handsome slave girls (jawarī) and young men slaves' (fityān). Slaving had become so profitable that Bornu's sovereign had to appeal to the Mamluks to rein in Egyptian and Syrian jullāb (slavers) to protect his subjects." (Gomez 2018:43) From the onset of Muslim entry into Bilād al sūdān, a negative perception existed within their worldview. Immediately we can see this in Battūta's account as he equates blacks with slaves. It could be argued that Battūta, a Moroccan helped influence Arab scholars, but that would be furthest from the truth; however, we will refer to Hall and Hunwick regarding other Arabic ideologies and ignorance.

An example of how Arabs used geographical locations to help them further draw distinctions between different Africans was the use of equatorial zones, which I mentioned early. A great example of that has been provided in Hunwicks' work. "The 1st zone is from the equator, extending to what lies beyond it and behind it. It contains the following nations: the Zanj, the Sūdān, the Habasha, and the Nūba, etc. Their blackness is due to the sun …Since its heat is extreme and it rises over them and is directly over their heads twice in a year, and remains close to them, it gives them a burning heat, and their hair, pursuant to the natural processes, becomes jet-black, curly and peppercorn-like, closely resembling hair that has been brought close to fire until it has become scorched. The most convincing proof that it is scorched is that it does not grow any longer. Their skins are hairless and smooth since the sun cleans the filth from their bodies and draws it out. Their brains have little humidity for similar reasons, and hence their intelligence is dim, their thoughts are not sustained, and their minds are inflexible, so that opposites, such as good faith and deceit, honesty and treachery, do not coexist among them. No divinely revealed laws have been found among them, nor has any divine messenger been sent among them, for they are incapable of handling opposites together, whereas divine laws consist of commanding and forbidding and creating desire and fear. The moral characteristics found in their belief systems are close to the instincts found naturally in animals, which require no learning to bring them out of the realm of potentiality into that of reality, like the braveness to be found in a lion, and the cunning in a fox."

(Hunwick & Powell 2009:36) The Arab world sees Africans as simply nothing more than a waste of human life; some even concluded that the 'Blacker they are, the uglier they are. Especially when it pertained to the Zanj and numerous West Africans. Arab scholarship didn't shy away from referring to one's character or disposition and assumed that the sharper the teeth, the more cannibalistic they were and dared to stay away from them. Arab racism went as far as to draw a line regarding sexual behaviors with the women due to their smell and bodies. All this energy spawns from the earlier mentioned 'Curse of Ham', which Arabs weaponized and alienated Blacks in Sudan. Regardless of Khaldūn's refutations of this curse, the myth was used to impact blacks negatively.

Numerous fables and tales began to be written about blacks so much so Abū Hāmid wrote, "In the land of the Sūdān exist people without heads. They are mentioned by al-Sha'bī in his book Siyar al-Mulūk. It is also said that in the deserts of the Magrib, there are a people of the progeny of Adam, consisting solely of women. There are no men among them, nor does any of the male sex life in that land. These women enter certain water by which they become pregnant. Each woman gives birth to a girl, never to a boy. Tubba' Dhū' l-Manār arrived in their country when he was trying to reach the Darkness (al-zulumāt), which Dhū' l-Qarnayn had entered. God knows best. And [it is also said] that his son, Ifrīqisūn, b Tudda' Dhū'l-Manār was the one who founded the town of Ifrīqiya, and called it after himself. And that his father, Tubba', reached Wādī al-Sabt (the River of Saturday), which is a river in the Maghreb, where sands flow like floodwater, and no living being may enter it without perishing. When he reached there, he hastened back. As for Dhū' l-Qarnayn, on his arrival there, he stayed until the day of Saturday, when the flow of the sand stopped, and then he crossed it and marched until he reached the Darkness. This is what is said, but God knows best. These headless people have eyes on their shoulders and mouths in their chests. They form many nations and are numerous like beasts. They reproduce and do not harm anyone, and they have no intelligence. God knows best." (Levtzion & Hopkins 2011:134) The Corpus of Early Arabic Sources is full of racist comments about Black Africans. The fictitious perspective of these so-called scholars is troubling when you consider the mindset of Arabs during the spread of Islam.

Every potential negative connotation that one person could bestow on another to justify their ignorance has been outlined and provided, making it easy to draw distinctions between how they viewed race and equated it with slavery. "Arabs had black Africans living among them before the days of Islam - mainly; it would appear as slaves." (Hunwick 2010:77) Some argue that Greeks, specifically Galileo influenced Arabic thought, but that seems furthest from the truth and honestly disingenuous among scholars who would institute that type of perspective. Blacks to Arabs constituted a class beneath them, which meant all the things Arabs didn't see fit to do, blacks were directed to do. Examples would be farming, tending to the land, and other things that constituted below them in the workforce arena. Early I had mentioned how Arabic perception validated North African views of Blacks in the case of Moroccans blacks to them equaled slavery. Another example of how race and slavery were infused on Blacks by Arabs is clear in Gomez's description: "Evidence for the articulation of slavery, race, and gender in the early Sahel makes an argument for change over time far more compelling than assumptions regarding the antiquity and pervasiveness of slavery. Slavery's development, however, would help shape views of West African women as well as concepts of blackness. Its expansion would also stimulate debate over human difference, and in ways not terribly removed from contemporary notions of race, resting on the fulcrum of an alleged, ancient curse." (Gomez 2019:57)

As far as the Moroccans who were familiar with West Africans below the Sahara, it has clearly been stated how they saw blacks as nothing more than slaves among them. "The slaves that Moroccans were consistently familiar with over the centuries were black Africans, and the view became widespread that they were 'natural' slaves. The Moroccan ruler Mūlāy Ismā'il (1668-1727) argued that all blacks resident in Morocco were unfree, being merely runaway slaves who had attached themselves to new patrons. He claimed they made good soldiers because they were naturally subservient and long-suffering. In fact, his pressed recruitment of blacks was indiscriminate, even including the harātīn - free, or freed, black men originally from northern Saharan oases who had migrated into Moroccan cities." (Hunwick & Powell 2009:42) This notion of blacks being slaves is unjust but expresses how Moroccans labeled blacks as mere slaves.

According to Hall: "Understanding how the concept of blackness gained instrumental value by the nineteenth century requires excavation of the intellectual developments within the field of Islamic legal literature of the Sahel in the seventeenth and eighteenth centuries. Racial ideas about blacks gained theoretical legal justification in this period, defining whole groups of people as permanently servile on the basis of genealogical arguments. Blackness came to define servile status." (Hall 2011:74).

I agree with Hall, especially when we have a Corpus of Early Arabic writing outlining how they perceived one's skin color and equated it to slavery and more. Those writings express distinction, ignorance, and attitudes towards people closer to and below the equator.

According to the National Institute of Health, Race by definition: "Race is a fluid concept used to group people according to various factors, including ancestral background and social identity. Race was also used to group people that share a set of visible characteristics, such as skin color and facial features. Though these visible traits are influenced by genes, the vast majority of genetic variation exists within racial groups and not between them. Race is an ideology, and for this reason, many scientists believe that race should be more accurately described as a social construct and not a biological one." (NIH 2020)

The Qur'ān even justifies color in it "3 (Āl' Imrān), 106: 'on a day, some faces will be whitened and some blackened. As for those whose faces are blacked (it will be said), 'Did you reject Faith after your belief in it?' Then taste the penalty for rejecting faith." (Hunwick 2010:89) What are we to make of this as the spread of Islam ravaged the hearts and minds of those they labeled Sūdānic. Black Africans had their own cultural and traditional systems and knew no Allah. So, how could they be held accountable for rejecting something that had absolutely no significance to them as a people? This seems to justify why Arab-Muslims used jihad to spread their beliefs. "The traditional Muslim ideology of slavery is closely linked to the doctrine of military jihad. Just as jihad is directed against non-belief in Islam, kufr, so the 'unbelievers,' kuffār captured in a jihad are the legally and religiously enslavable in Muslim society. The Qur'an in this regard admonishes Muslims thus: 'When you meet the unbelievers [ina jihad], smite their necks, then, when you have made wide slaughter among them, tie fast the bonds [of slavery]'. The victorious Muslim ruler could then choose either to free his captives out of generosity (presumably after their conversion to Islam), or in exchange for a ransom." (Azumah 2020:125)

"The equivalence of blackness of skin with slavery continues to be reflected in the Arabic dialects spoken by many Arabs; i.e., 'avid = blacks. In 1995 in Nigeria, when I was speaking in Arabic with a Lebanese, he simply referred to Nigerians as 'abīd, and modern dictionary of Egyptian spoken Arabic also defines 'abd first as 'slave,' and secondly as negro." (Hunwick 2010:88) No matter how hard Black Africans attempted to idealize and accept Islam, the line in the sand continues to be drawn. According to Hunwick regarding Al - Baydāwī's comments: 'Whiteness of skin and blackness of it, or the layout of limbs and their shapes and colors, and their quality, so that there occur distinctions and recognition until there is a difference in dual harmonizing together with the conformity of their materials and the matters encountered by the two of them in smoothing [massaging?] Although these quotations seem to condemn black Africans, it is quite evident that many black Africans who converted to Islam have been true worshippers of God and acting in respect of all orders of the Qur'an." (Hunwick 2010:89) Equality under any circumstance could not be reached, and Arab scholars continued to make these distinctions in their writings. "Blackness gained legal meaning in the seventeenth and eighteenth centuries in the Sahel. By the beginning of the nineteenth century, Muslim scholars in the region had accumulated a set of theoretical legal tools that could be used to render blacks inferior to nonblacks. The importance of these developments is evident in the case of the forgery of the 'Ta'rīkh al-fattāsh,' an important seventeenth-century chronicle of the history of the Niger Bend. A skilled nineteenth-century scholar loyal to Amadu Lobbo, the founder of the reformist Islamic State called the Hamdullahi Caliphate, inserted racial categories into the original chronicle to mark off permanent servile status groups of people defined as black slaves. By doing this, the scholar provided Amadu Lobbo with the justification for arguments he made about his authority over the people of the Niger Bend. The forged 'Ta'rīkh al-fattāsh' shows us some of the important work that the theorization of collective racial categories could perform by the nineteenth century." (Hall 2011:69-70) Hall refers to manuscript C, and modern scholarship has exposed this error and tends to disregard that transcript as not credible. However, we have a section of pseudo-historians on social media who try to use that manuscript to argue for Jews' existence in certain parts of West Africa, among other things. Lobbo knew what he was doing in manipulating that manuscript; he wanted to rewrite history to continue Arab supremacy in an area full of resources that enriched Arabs and justified their racist behavior towards blacks.

In conclusion: Arabs used many different distinctions and cultural influences to associate color with race. From the equatorial assertions and Curse of Ham, along with the mere classist ideology of Blacks in their eyes, it was no way that Blacks could ever be equal to them due to the complexion of their skin. Arabs equated blackness with being uncivilized and unjust. We see examples of this in history as Blacks were used as slaves to build Arab supremacy. Overall Muslim apologists act as if this is not a reality and sweep this under the rug to proselytize and romanticize Islam as a saving tool to bring them out of a dark state that racist whites forced upon them. Not much is mentioned regarding the Trans-Saharan kidnapping of our Ancestors, and that is because to reap the benefits of trade, one must overlook the injustices and role that Islam allowed in Bīlād al-Sūdān. It was set in motion from its initial onset that blacks, in their own words, were indeed slaves, culturally different, and inferior to Arabs and those who looked similar in complexion to them. Their prejudices started from a bible and grew culturally as its wickedness expanded. By the time Islam reached the interior of Bilād al-Sūdān, it had been recognized as the gift West Africa could bestow on its control. This would further provoke their ignorance and conjecture, which would explain precisely how Arabs invoked race with slavery and use it as a tool to control the hearts and minds of many today!

Chapter Five
The Claim - Did Islam Come In Peace?
A response to Lord Abba

"Briefly summarized, Islam ('submission' to the will of God) originated in the Arabian Peninsula when the Prophet Muhammad (b. c.570; d. 632) began to receive his first revelations from God, via the Angel Gabriel, in about 610. Initially, Muslim converts were few, but by 615, Muhammad could be regarded as the leader of a community (Lapidus 1988:25). This community was established in Mecca (contemporary Saudi Arabia), but owing to difficult conditions there, Muhammad and his followers moved to Medina in 622 (also in Saudi Arabia), in an event known as the hijrah or migration, and forming Year One of the Muslim calendar (1 AH, al-hajrah). With this move, the formal establishment of the Muslim community, ummah, can be considered to have taken place. Conflict with the non-Muslim Meccans continued until an armistice was signed in 628, and in 630, the Muslim occupation of Mecca was completed. In 632, the Prophet died in Medina, where he was buried (Lapidus 1988; Waines 1995, Insoll 1999a).

To establish the basis of the argument, we must understand how Islam formed before its spread. To add, Muhammad did not create Islam; it predates him, and he would be considered just one of many Prophets, in this case, the last who would guide humanity. "Muhammad is thus not the founder of Islam, a religion that already existed, but the last in the chain of the prophets, being the 'Seal of the prophets' (khātimu l-anbiyā). Islam venerates all preceding prophets as messengers of God's will." (Fasi 1992:16) So the influence of a religion created outside of Africa that started year one in Medina under the reign of its last Prophet Muhammad saw very few converts earlier on. This point is significant because it stresses that even though its inception was in Saudi Arabia as we know of it today had very little influence on the cultural worldview of Arabians.

Historically, the relevance Islam poses to Africa is through trade, and that trade occurred across the Red Sea. So, Africans earliest encounter with Islam was due to a disruption in trade and Abyssinian influence in the region' (Willis 1971:137). "The progress of Islam in its first century was swift; Muslim power in Arabia was rapidly consolidated and under the successors to Muhammad the Khalifahs or Rightly Guided Caliphs, the Muslim armies spread into and conquered Palestine, Iraq, Syria, large parts of Iran, and Egypt between 633 - 650. These initial conquests were shortly followed by others under subsequent dynasties; between 674 and 715, a Muslim Central Asian frontier zone was established with the conquest of Transoxania, and by the end of the first quarter of the eighth century, the conquest of the Maghreb (North Africa) and al-Andalus (Islamic Spain) was complete (Lapidus 1988). Thus Islam was established in the Arabian Peninsula across the Red Sea from Africa, North of the Sahara in parts of the Maghreb and Egypt, all three areas bordering or adjacent to parts of sub-Saharan Africa with which we are concerned." (Insoll 2003:12)

The spread of Islam was swift and decisive; as stated above, conquest helped establish the presence of Islam in areas that had been very unfamiliar with it like Ethiopia, Kemet, The Maghreb, Spain, and more. What I find difficult to comprehend is that Lord Abba makes this assertion claiming to have used Timothy Insoll as a reference point in his YouTube lecture while educating the masses on Islam and more. Once an army amassed, the spread of Islam as peaceful goes out of the window. So, the argument shifts gears, and as expected, a believer ignores the evidence to justify his faith in what seems to be an identity crisis.

"Islam spread from the Arabian Peninsula by virtue of the jihad Muhammad's followers declared upon his enemies. Despite its popular conception, the jihad, another fundamental duty in Islam, involves much more than 'holy war' waged to expand Islamic frontiers or to defend the faith against foreign intrusion. For the believer, jihad is a form of effort - 'a struggle in the path of Allah' - that can be undertaken by peaceful or military means.

In short, the diffusion of Islam was viewed by Muslims as a serious effort to be undertaken for Allah's sake, as indeed the Crusades were launched by Christians' for the glory of God' and the protection of His Church." (Willis 1971:140-141)

Also, "Two things at the beginning of Islam caused them to (fight in closed formation). First, their enemies fought in closed formation, and that forced them to fight that way. Second, they were willing to die in the holy war because they wished to prove their endurance and were very firm in their belief. Now, the closed formation is the fighting technique most suitable for one willing to die." (Rosenthal, Dawood 2005:226) Islamists prepared to die to spread their religion, so it is highly romanticized if someone argued differently. Lord Abba seems unaware of its historical narrative and attacks on those who did not subscribe to Allah.

If Islam was to spread in peace, how could we justify Muhammads' last raid? 'An example of the was the Muslim dynasty when God united power of the Arabs in

Islam. The number of Muslims who participated in the raid against Tabuk, the Prophet's last raid, was 110,000 Mudar and Qahatan horseman and foot soldiers. That number was augmented by those who became Muslims after the (raid) and down to the time of the Prophet's death. When (all these people) then set out to seek for themselves the royal authority held by (other) nations, there was no protection against them or refuge. They were allowed (to take possession of) the realms of the Persians and the Byzantines, who were the greatest dynasties in the world at that time (as well as the realms) of the Turks in the East, of the Goths in Spain. They went from the Hijaz to as-Sus in the far West and Yemen to the Turks in the far North. They gained possession of all seven zones." (Rosenthal, Dawood, Lawrence 2005:129-30) The wrath of Islam spread by the sword, and it's evident when the European Christians in north Africa rebelled when Arabs forced their religion upon them; however, that led to Muslims massacring them.

"The wars of expansion of the Islamic State after the death of the Prophet were not aimed at the conversion of the conquered people since the majority of these adhered to religions with revealed scriptures, such as the Christians, Zoroastrians, and Jews. They were obliged to pay the poll tax (djizya) and then became protected (dhimmī) without being forced to abandon their religion. The essential aim was the expansion of the Islamic State as the sphere within which the sharī'a was paramount. This came to be expressed in the distinctions between Dār al-Islām and Dār al-Harb, the sphere of Islam and the sphere of war." (Fasi 1992:24) Understanding sharī'a became critical information because if you practiced one of the three major religions mentioned, you could continue the practice of that religion if you paid your fees. If you did not adhere to the following, a conversion would occur, or jihad war was inevitable.

Muhammad said: 'War is trickery' An Arab proverb says: 'Many a trick is worth more than a tribe.' (Rosenthal, Dawood, Lawrence 2005:229) It is evident that Muhammad had a grasp for tricky, especially within the war, because this would allow him to deceive his enemies and conquer them. If the spread of Islam were about peace, it wouldn't be a need for trickery amid saving souls who he believed were doomed in the eyes of his faith. I find it quite interesting that an Arab proverb would influence trickery that says a lot about what converts would endure in their conversion to Islam. "It is thus clear that superiority in war is, as a rule, the result of hidden causes, not of external ones. The occurrence of opportunities resulting from hidden causes is what is meant by the word' luck.' This explains Muhammad's victory with small numbers over the polytheists during his lifetime and the victories of the Muslims during the Muslim conquests after Muhammad's death. Terror in the hearts of their enemies was why there were so many routes during the Muslim conquests, but it was a factor concealed from men's eyes." (Rosenthal, Dawood, Lawrence 2005:229)

In the early history of Islam, most Arabs were not allowed to step foot on African soil; as Insoll states: 'Until the tenth century, Muslims were largely confined to the coast and offshore islands such as Dahlak Kebir. From this date, trade, allied with proselytization, were the vital factors in the spread of Islam away from coastal areas.' (Insoll 2003:58) Archeology supports this, which makes Insoll important regarding Lord Abba because had he read the complete work, he would understand that peacefully is romanticized. African American converts who hide under the veil of Noble Drew Ali and the Moorish movement do not adequately understand how the spread of Islam occurred. Abba professes to be a researcher and scholar of the modern-day Youtube Conscious world, yet he failed to refer to the data and draw an honest conclusion.

"According to the Arabic historical sources, the first Muslim contacts with the western Sahel were undertaken by Kharijites, namely, Ibadi merchants (Lewicki 1960, 1962, 1964, 1971). Among the earliest recorded contacts are those between Ibadi

Imamate of Tahert (in modern Algeria) and Gao, soon after the foundation of Tahert in the late eighth century. There are various other references to trade relations between Tahert and the western Sahel between the mid-ninth and early tenth centuries. For example, Ibn as-Saghir, the chronicler of Tahert, wrote at the beginning of the tenth century that a notable of the city, Muhammad inn 'Arfa, stayed at the court of a king of the Sudan (a reference to the western Sahel region). During his stay, he acted as an ambassador for the Ibadi Rostemid Imam of Tahert, who ruled between 823 and 872. Although this Sudanese ruler is not mentioned by name, (Lewicki 1971:119) makes the point that it is conceivable that this envoy was sent to the ruler of either Ghana or Gao. Similarly, Ibaedi sources also refer to trade with Tadmekka (Lewicki 1971:117), probably to be identified with the site of Essuk in Mali (Farias 1900)." (Insoll 2003:214)

Based on the above quotation, we can conclude that Arabs, not Africans, made contact with people in modern Algeria and Gao around the tenth century. So no presence of Islam or Muslims existed in the foothills of Bilad al-Sudan at this point, and we will uncover just how Islam pranced into West Africa and how it spread like wildfire. From the onset of my argument, nothing peaceful about the spread of Islam exists. The moment you impose your ideology on a people, you have mentally committed an act of psychological warfare against them. That is not an act of peace or solidarity; that is an act with the intent to enforce your ideology on strangers for the greater good of yourself. We will revisit this behavior and expand on it in the coming chapters. Arabs felt superior over Africans at the onset of its Islamic expansion; they felt the need to see them as inferior and infidels because they did not know of Muhammad or practice the ways of its Prophet. Let's be more specific Islam was brought by Berbers of North Africa via the Middle East. To be more precise, The Massufa clan, who were Sanhaja roamed around the Sahara as nomads. It would later settle near Gao, looking for opportunities to capitalize on cross Saharan trade. It is also said that these Bidans (whites) would decide near the Takedda region and also Timbuktu. "Importantly for them, the Berber populations of their occupied territories mostly converted to Islam. In this way, Islam passed on to Saharan nomads, particularly the Berber Sanhaja of the western Sahara. With the renewal and growth of their faith in the mid-eleventh century, the Sanhaja formed a movement known as the Almoravids (al-Murābitūn), which then occupied all of the regions of modern Morocco and moved into the area of Spain overtaken by Arab Muslims. As widespread Saharan nomads, their faith to Islam soon began to have an influence on West African 'black' populations." (Hunwick 2006:25)

Conversion to Islam was not all about blood or peace; it was brokered by trade and commerce, and to take part in this trade, many people converted. "The historical records indicate that Islam was not long confined to nomad and mercantile contexts.

By the late tenth and early eleventh centuries they record a new phenomenon - that conversions, not of traders but of local rulers, were beginning to take place." (Insoll 2003:224) Many, like the Takrur, used the new religion for political gain and forced it upon its people. Many who experienced servitude saw Islam as a way out of debt and took the opportunity to convert. So, it also seems that conversion took shape by a form of personal interest for many.

"In the commercial centers of the Sahel the North African Muslim traders came in contact with two elements of the local population: with the Sudanese traders between the termini of the trans-Saharan trails and the gold sources, and the with the rulers of the Sudanese states, who controlled the trade. Islam began to win converts among traders and rulers, and for a long time, it was limited to these two influential elements. On the other hand, Islam left the little impression among the stateless peoples or the commoners, whose way of life had hardly been changed by their incorporation into the political framework of the states. Patterns of trade and of political

organization conditioned the spread of Islam, while on the other hand, Islam played an important role in the fortunes of the Sudanese states, both as an external force (Ghana facing the Almoravids) and as an internal factor of cohesion or disintegration. The history of Western Sudan revolves, therefore, around these three themes: trade, states, and Islam." (Levtzion 1972:124)
"Initially converted rulers in the Sahel region were those contacted by Muslim merchants from North Africa, and they obtained items for trading with them, notably non-Muslims seized as slaves, both male and female. Hence elements of 'black Africa (bilād al-sūdān) became elements of 'Arab' Africa. Some of them converted to Islam, which led to their being freed, though many then remained in 'Arab' Africa. In Morocco, many 'black' Africans were put into a military force in the early eighteenth century, on the assumption that all were slaves." (Hunwick 2010:28)

Arab interest in the West is evident it was not about the spread of Islam; it was about the gold that the Saudi's enjoyed and every other Arab in the area. Levtzion writes: "The Arab conquest on North Africa gave the trans-Saharan trade a new impetus by linking it with a vast empire, anxious to obtain as much as possible of its gold, on which the monetary system of the Muslim world depended." (Levtzion 1972:122) Understanding this point would also influence one to wreak havoc over a people to control its resources and establish itself in the lands. As the layers of scholarship reveal the Arabs' intent to spread Islam, we began to see just how dangerous conversion had to be for West Africans and others why conversion seems necessary at times for certain Chiefs or Kings. "The question can be posed as to why then the ruler of Ghana tolerated Muslims, apparently in large numbers, at his capital. One suggested reason has been that administration was improved through the use of Arabic (in what were pre-literate contexts) as well as through using Muslim officials (Dramani-Issifou 1992:57). This would appear to be supported by the historical sources, as al-Bakri also recorded that the King's interpreters, the official in charge of his treasury, and the majority of his ministers are Muslims' (Levtzion and Hopkins 1981:80). These are also reasons why the non-Muslim Asante rulers allowed a substantial Muslim presence in their capital. Equally, it could be asked why a ruler might convert to Islam when he had a divine status or was what Mbiti (1975:161) describes as God's earthly representative. Numerous suggestions can be made to account for this - genuine belief, or the addition it could make to the panoply of ritual, perhaps. Levtzion (1979:214) makes the point in this respect that among Muslims with little or no Islamic education, the ritual rather than the legal aspects of Islam was of greater importance." (Insoll 2003:226)

Similar to Europeans, Arabs made dealing with them seem just as if they had all the tools and means to help Africans achieve what seemed unattainable in some instances. They wanted agency over their rivals and a continuum of power and presence among their tribe. Having a seat in the afterlife next to Allah and control over enslaving rival tribes became justifiable. The influence of gold also drove Arabs to partake in setting up small pockets of power along with trade rights so that they could dictate trade and commerce and enrich themselves along the way.

Once Islam entered some regions of West Africa, people began to disperse, going in many directions to reframe from conversion. Those who stayed played prominent roles in expanding Islam and monitoring trade routes. "Even after these attempts to consolidate its strength, Islam was by no means generally accepted. It became the religion of small communities of traders and professional clerics." (Fasi 1972:43) When Islam encountered setbacks, jihad was used, and blood was drawn because it was sharia (law) that determined it was lawful to commit this hideous act on non-converts. Not everyone converted; you had the Mossi and others who rejected Islam withstood jihad attempts by the legendary Askia Muhammad and others, but that fight wore on them over time, causing conversion later on down the line.

In conclusion: the spread of Islam in Africa began in the East and gradually made its way to the North into the West via converts who saw themselves differently as those in Bilad al-Sudan. Conversion occurred in a multitude of ways that included forced and non-forced conversions. Some converted for political gain others converted to escape slavery. Those who helped spread Islam saw fit to involve themselves in trade which provided a pathway for riches and power that non-converts would not experience. "The western Sahel was the first point of Muslim contact in West Africa, and it can be seen, as on the Red Sea and East African coasts, that the archaeology of Islam in this region is again initially trade-related in origins and development. From the late eighth century, intermittent contacts through the agency of trans-Saharan trade took a couple of centuries to develop into anything sizable. Yet it was also evident that conversion to Islam was by no means instantaneous, and it proved possible to advance a general model to account for this process in this region, charting the spread of Islam through various socio-economic groups - traders, nomads, rulers, urban dwellers and agriculturists." (Insoll 2003:260-261)

Islam was not this pretty person that commanded a room and grabbed everyone's attention. It was ugly, and scholars wrote to romanticize themselves as saviors and golden boys. They pranced around converting non-believers acting as missionaries of Allah, and they used racial stereotypes and biblical narratives to excuse their actions as they felt justified by their actions.

In volume 2 of From Spears to Pens, brother Sutekh and I touched on the overly racist Arabs. "E.W. Bovill (1968:93) made the point about the famous fourteenth-century Moroccan traveller Ibn Battuta that 'he had hardly arrived [in western Sudan] before he was regretting having come, merely because he was disgusted at finding Negroes, whom hitherto he had known only as slaves, behaving as masters in their own country." (Insoll 2003:232) Many see Battuta as a world-renowned traveler who African American Moors hold in high regard to thinking that his traveler was disgusted speaks to how they viewed blacks. "The inherent racial bias that is present in many of the writings, also to be found in other sources such as Victorian explorers account] must be remembered when these sources are being used as an aid in interpretation and reconstruction." (Insoll 2003:232) Arabs disrespected Africans, let alone how they used their culture to impose itself on others by blood. Especially in the times of Muhammad when he used an army for their mini-wars, and then jihad became a staple of its presence as it spread.

So, it is safe to say that brother Abba never considered the onslaught of evidence compiled by modern and recent scholarship that dealt with the question extensively. Islam was not our friend; it became the enemy the day East Africans held Arabs at bay in the Red Sea when it came to trade. It was the enemy when the Moroccans filtered into West Africa, dangling carrots in the faces of Kings and Chiefs. It was the enemy when Africans had to run to the bush in fear of losing their identity but, most importantly, mainly losing their lives. A lot of African blood is on the hands-on Islam, and in no way can we conclude that it came to us in peace.

Chapter Six
The Spread of Islam Meant Controlling The Trade

"Islam, which had spread on the fringes of the continent, now penetrated it much more deeply and became firmly established. Muslim Arab traders linked into a multi-continental network were replaced by African traders who penetrated deep into the forest zones." - D.T. Niane

"Islam, which had spread on the fringes of the continent, now penetrated it much more deeply and became firmly established. Muslim Arab traders linked into a multi-continental network were replaced by African traders who penetrated deep into the forest zones." - D.T. Niane "Most histories date the beginnings of trans-Saharan trade to sometime after the arrival of Islam in North Africa, during the seventh century CE. But the fifth-century BCE Greek author Herodotus describes a trade route from Egypt far into the desert during his own lifetime." (Austen 2010:1) Austen would direct us to a series of questions surrounding Herodotus' claim of a trade route from Egypt deep into the desert. Still, he also hints at specifics trying to understand the human struggle with the Sahara because it is the largest desert in the world and is always dry, hot, and difficult to travel without familiarity.

We know that before Europeans came, the outside world had no contact with people below the Sahara. In my previous work, I spoke to that point regarding speculation around Mali-Koi Kan-Kan Mūsā. Scholars have, in a sense, argued about pre-Islamic trade between Egypt and West Africans, citing glass beads, cowrie shells, cultural nuisances, and more. That topic is debated in certain circles on social media platforms such as Facebook and YouTube. However, this is about Islam and the importance of that seventh-century presents and dominance by Arabs via trade. Within this realm and among certain Arab scholars, trade flourished, creating an immense amount of wealth for Arabs as history romanticized Islamic presence and status in Africa.

"The trans-Saharan trade was not a timeless phenomenon. It arose, developed, and underwent major changes, which we need to study as best we can. From the point of view of this trade, the seventh - eleventh centuries were of crucial importance. It was at this period that regular links grew up between the Mediterranean economies, with their demand particularly for gold, and those of the Saharan Sahel and the savannas linking it to the forest region, which used salt but produced little of it. But it has long been moot point how far back these crossings go." (Devisse 1992:190)

From what we know about our North African counterparts who looked down to the blacks below the Sahara, they seem to be familiar with an earlier presence regarding routes into Bilād al-Sūdān. We know them as the Berbers who seem to dominate trade routes earlier own into ladder parts of recent history. The Berbers were Uber drivers of the Sahara, and the camels served the best purpose in the desert. "Historians of ancient North Africa are not entirely sure whether relations between its Mediterranean and Saharan regions extended beyond the desert to include trade with the Western and Central Sudan. On balance, available evidence suggest that no significant level of such commerce - or perhaps none at all - took place before the arrival of Arab conquerors in the seventh century CE. But the arguments on the other side - even those with the least foundation - are still worth exploring for what they say about the difficulties of moving beyond the geographical barrier of the post-Neolithic Sahara." (Austen 2010:11)

So, from the Arab perspective, trade was irrelevant until its presence, and West Africa was outside until Islam made them relevant. This mindset was the focal point of Arabs in their writings and attitude toward the people in Bilād al-Sūdān. So, what about the evidence found regarding the Sudanic gold trade and the Romans? It seems that Arabic sources have no recollections of this event taking place. Yet, in the Eighth Century, we know that Arabs raided Western Sahara looking for gold and other valuable exports. According to Herodotus, the one main item that continued to come up was salt; he raved about the blocks of salt that could be extracted from Western Sahara, and during those times, salt had more value than gold. Pre-Islamic trade, according to historians, is somewhat limited, and the presence of trade from west of the Sahara with the rest of the world is rarely mentioned.

"The penetration of Islam into the Western and Central Sudan depended on its power to link different groups of people. Yet the first merchants to organize regular trans-Saharan trade were dissidents Muslims. During the first century and a half of Islamic presence (680-800), major sectarian and ethnic divisions plagued the Maghrib. The Arab rulers of this period came from a culture that was closer to that of the Berbers than had their Roman, Vandal, and Byzantine predecessors. Like these earlier regimes, however, they imposed heavy taxes on their North African subjects. The terms of submission Uqba imposed on the regions he subdued in the central Sahara included the supply of hundreds of slaves, and this demand continued throughout the region under his successors." (Austen 2010:21) We know what would come of the Berbers' oppression when Islam spread. That would lead them directly to conversion and accepting some form of Islam that would help expand the Arabs role in North Africa and provide them with an opportunity to expand their residency and presence in the area.

With this new presence, Arabs would establish important roles in parts of North Africa as it spread, allowing them to create a residency in crucial areas in the Sudan where trade routes would evolve. "The Kharijite settlements in the Sahara provide a recorded beginning point for regular trans-Saharan trade on a significant scale. The combination of economic enterprise and nonaggressive Islamic religious practice that characterized both the Ibadis and the Moroccan Sufris also produced a model for the peaceful linkage of Mediterranean civilization to the Sudanic world. The era of the Sahara as a barrier now ended, and its role as a global highway began." (Austen 2010:22)

Keep in mind that Arabs were obsessed with gold from the jump, and the more gold that could be extracted and sent back to the Muslim world, the better. "West Africa is rich in easily workable mineral deposits." (Frye 1972:239) Resources made it very attractive to Muslim traders looking for advantages in the Mediteranean, among other things. "Arabic sources provide the earliest contemporary evidence about the trade and stat4es that flourished in Western Sudan before 1500. Al-Fazārī, writing towards the end of the eighth century, describes the extensive kingdom of 'Ghana, the land of gold." (Levztion 1972:120) They saw West Africa as its Fort Knox, and by any means necessary, they set in motion a political agenda that would help them establish the presence needed to control the gold.

"When writing about West African gold, most of the Muslim authors employ the word tibr which is commonly translated as 'gold dust.' In reality, this term has the meaning of 'native, untreated and unminted gold,' in every case gold in the rough state as opposed to worked gold (Arab. Dhahab). It is only by taking into account this precise meaning of tibr that we can interpret correctly the many texts alluding to this kind of gold in West Africa." (Devisse 1992:195) Al-bakrī has been quoted as saying that the gold in West Africa is the best globally; also, Muslims have stated that it was the purest they have ever seen. But during the middle to late 10th Century Muslims did not contain a proper stronghold in the South over the gold in Bilād al-Sūdān, which would soon change the more Islam began to spread. Gold would put Ghana in the spotlight because it contained immense wealth. Trade routes were established at two key intersectional stages of the gold trade. It possessed a King who took full advantage of expanding his kingdom in areas that would benefit Ghana and allow it to thrive and become one of the leading gold importers in the area.

"Ghana was also the center for the export trade in copper, mined in the Sahara regions, and was also the center of the trade-in desert salt. In the Sahara, there were large deposits of hard rock salt, which was quarried for export, cut into large slabs like building blocks. Indeed at Taghaza, the main salt mine in the middle of the desert, about five hundred miles north of Timbuktu, the houses were all built of salt blocks, roofed with camel skins. From Taghaza the salt trade went south to Ghana and north to the cities of North Africa." (Frye 1972:243-44)

Due to Ghana's geographical location, it set the stage for what most people call go-betweens. Those middlemen would be Jenne, Gao, and Timbuktu, who all grew into large cities and established themselves as traders who took advantage of the opportunities Ghana presented them. From the outside looking in, you'd think that Africans dominated this trade wholeheartedly. Some would argue that this was indeed an African trade, but beneath that, the presence of Muslims was everywhere. According to al-Bakri, before the fall of Ghana, Islam would have a strong footprint in Western Sudan.

As Basil Davidson states: "From this account of Al-Bakri's, one can guess a good deal of what had happened during earlier times. It appears that many of the North African and Berber traders of the Sahara accepted Islam after the Arab conquest of the eighth century. They abandoned their old religions and became Muslims. They were made welcome at the capital of the emperor of Ghana, who was not a Muslim but a believer in Ghana's own religion, probably the religion of the Soninke, and were allowed to build a town of their own. The 'town of the Muslim traders' was six miles away from the emperor's own town with its surrounding settlements. While the latter were built in the traditional materials of West Africa - hardened clay, thatch, and wooden beams - the more successful Muslim traders preferred to build their houses in stone, according to their own customs in North Africa. It is not exactly known where the capital was when Al-Bakri wrote his book. In the course of Ghana's long history, the king's capital was undoubtedly moved from one place to another. But we can add a good deal to Al-Bakri's picture by studying the remains of Ghana's last capital, which lay at Kumbi Saleh about two hundred miles north of modern Bamako. Here too there was a town where the king of Ghana lived, and another nearby town where the Muslim traders had their houses and stables. At the height of its prosperity, before AD 1240, this city of Kumbi was evidently the biggest West African City of its day, and may have had as many as fifteen thousand inhabitants or even more." (Davidson 1966:41-42) As I mentioned before, Muslims established themselves in areas where they could oversee, run, and manipulate trade in areas of Bilād al-Sūdān that would benefit regardless of the wealth blacks created for themselves. This exact blueprint that Basil Davidson describes in Ghana transpired in numerous countries in West Africa. The philosophical ideology of Muslims consists of merchants who broker deals that allow them to accumulate wealth off-trade, pretty much a tax, so whatever deals that transpired in the market area Allah the merciful would need his fare like Uncle Sam in America per-say. Maps regarding trade routes created and designed by Arab scholars provided valuable intel regarding multiple directions in and out of Ghana and ventured into many directions. When it comes to the Spread of Islam and who controlled what in which area, we can conclude that when it comes to West Africa, we rely heavily on external sources to paint the picture of what life was like during the reign of Ghana, Timbuktu, Gao, Jenne, Mali and so forth.

Understanding the basis allows Muslims to claim that West Africa would not have been what it once was, but at the same time, one can argue without the Spread of Islam and the presence of Muslims, it would not be what it is today. That is another argument for another day; however, West Africans did thrive regardless of Muslims' role. It would be a role 'New Enemies' would assume in the coming centuries that would broker the Trans-Atlantic holocaust and send West Africa into a state of psychological and cultural disarray.

Chapter: Seven Bilad al Bidan
White Rule in Ancient West Africa

The history of West Africa is the long story of human movements, incursions, displacements, intermixtures, or successions of people, and the impact of these on the beliefs, attitudes, and social organization of the various peoples who today inhabit this great area." (Mabogunje 1971:1) Scientists have argued in the journal of scientific advances that archaic hominids populated West Africa a million years ago, but the earliest homo-sapien was found in Morocco some 300,000 years ago.

In Nigeria, specifically, Iwo Eleru scientist found a human skull that dates back some 11,200 years. 'Tiny fragments of charcoal, accompanied by Old Stone Age tools, recovered from tin-workings near Jos on the Nigerian plateau, suggest when submitted to scientific methods of dating, an age 'greater than 39,000 years.' Whether Negroes or Negroid peoples were living in West Africa and in the Sahara too at that time is not known, but it is believed that they existed in the area around 5000 BC Rock paintings and engravings recently discovered by Henri Lhote, a French archaeologist, indicate that Negroes, presumably from West Africa and its neighborhood, had been living as far as the Tassil plateau in the Sahara before 3000 BC' (Ifemesia 1973:40).

"Four West African populations carry genes from what may be an undiscovered archaic hominin. This archaic group of humans seems likely to have diverged from the shared ancestor of Neanderthals, Denisovans, and modern humans before these lineages split about 800,000 years ago." (Ackerly 2020) Recently in Cameroon, a burial site was excavated; its findings uncovered more available data. "For the first time, scientists analyzed the ancient genetics of four individuals from the Shum Laka rock shelter in western Cameroon. The samples came from two burials at the site, one roughly 3,000 years ago and another around 8,000 years ago." (Wei-Hass 2020) It is safe to say that West Africa has its own story that has yet to be fully written about like other parts of Africa, and once it has been presented on a global stage, its genius will be forever remembered.

Science is having its say genetically on the orientation of West Afrikans, while historians of the past were not afforded the right to have this type of technological advancement to help them write or be descriptive in their eye witness accounts.

Knowing what we know today, it is safe to say that within 2.4 million square miles West Africa was inhabited by a people who recent history tends to say: 'was barbaric, uncivilized, pagans, and had no cultural identity to build the great civilizations that existed a few hundred years ago.'

Who ruled Bilad al-Sudan will be argued later; however, we need to keep one thing in mind while it comes to the thought process of early historians and or people in general. "Since the whole of the southern half of Africa was unknown to Arab merchants and travelers, except for East African coast which, for them ran due east from Cape Gardafui [present-day Somalia], it was represented as being essentially uninhabited. This posited lack of population was explained by the fact that the farther south went beyond the equator, the hotter the climate became. Even in the 'land of the blacks' just north of the equator, people's brain 'almost boiled form the heat,' as one author puts it. (Al-Dimashqi) See: (Hopkins & Levtzion 2011:205) People were presumed not to be able to live in heat more intense than that; ergo, there could be no people living south of the equator, and to some extent, the second clime to the north of it, was thought to affect both body color and intelligence. Extreme cold in the seventh clime in northern Europe was thought to have similar effects, bleaching skins, and numbing brains!" (Hunwick 2005:110)

These are the thoughts of Arab (Muslim) scholars while they were documenting Africans who lived below the equator. I find it very interesting that Al-Dimashqi states: 'The equator is inhibited by communities of the Sudan who may be numbered among the savage beast. Their complexions and hair are burnt, and they are physically and morally abnormal.' (Levtzion & Hopkins 2011:205)

Immediately we can take into account the displeasure Arabs have for the people of Sudan. With confidence, they write about Black Africans as if they are nothing more than beasts whose physical and moral perspectives are inhumane. This is very important to know because this perspective will continue to dominate one's worldview based on written historical accounts. Let's deal with a renowned scholar by the name of Al-Bakri as he informs us of how Islam made its way west and his perspective of the Sanghana people.

"The City of Sanghana consists of two towns standing on either bank of the Nil. Its habitations reach the ocean. The town of Sanghana is close on the south-western side of that of Takrur, also situated on the Nil. The inhabitants are Sudan, who previously, like all the other Sudan, pagans, and worshipped dakakir (dakkur is their word for an idol) until Warjabi b Rabis became their ruler. He embraced Islam, introduced among them Muslim religious laws, and compelled them to observe it, thus opening their eyes to the truth. Warjabi died in the year 432/1040

—41, and the people of Takrur are Muslims today." (Levtzion & Hopkins 2011:77)

Muslim scholar Ibn Khaldun writes: 'We have seen that Negros are in general characterized by levity, excitability, and great emotionalism. They are found to dance wherever they hear a melody. They are everywhere described as stupid.' (Hunwick 2005:128) Account after account, we will find some slight or insult hurled at the description of Blacks in Africa.

"Some writers attempted to justify certain stereotypes with 'scientific' support based on zodiacal and planetary influences or, rather later, with theories about the influence of climate on skin color and temperament. As an example of the zodiacal/planetary school of thought, we may take the tenth-century geographer Al-Hamdani (d.945), who claims for his theories an origin in the writing of Ptolemy. The world may be divided into four sectors, each of which comprises three zodiacal signs influenced by one of the four elements: fire, earth, air and water. In this scheme, sub-Saharan Africa lies in the fourth or south-western quadrant, which comprises Cancer, Scorpio and Pisces and is under the influence of the elements water. Ghana and what he called 'the land of the naked blacks' is modeled on the triad of Cancer and are under the influence of Venus and Mars." (Hunwick 2005:124) The audacity to use pseudoscience to propagate his hatred or dislike for the blacks is merely laughable. We are witnessing the racial bias of scholars that have had a major impact on scholarship from the past several hundred years.

When we look back at the earliest writings in 'Bilad al Sudan,' we tend to get the perspective of Muslim travelers and chroniclers who wrote detailed accounts about the latest history of West Africa and West Afrikans. Chronicles such as the Ta'rikh al-Fattash and the Ta'rikh al Sudan speak of great empires, conflicts, plagues, and adventures in parts of Jenne, Timbuktu, Gao, Songhai, Mali, Kano, and more. Mahmud Kati, Al-Bakri, and Al-Sa'di's and a few others are responsible for the worldview on West Afrikan history. Not to dismiss the most notable traveler Ibn Battuta and others who left countless chronicles for us to learn from. But, it is Al-Sa'di's Ta'rikh al-Sudan that we encounter the mention of the Bidan and the account of al-Hasan b Muhammad al-Wazzan al-Zayyati who also writes about the Bidan ruling West Afrika. I believe that racism fueled this, and for numerous years it began to be regurgitated by racist Muslims and Europeans who sought to write black Afrikans out of the history books.

Before we deal with al-Hasan b Muhammad al-Wazzan al-Zayyati and his account. I want to address something mentioned in the Ta'rikh al-Sudan by Al-Sa'di's. He rights in chapter four of his work about Mali and its provinces.

"Observation. Mali is a very large and extensive region in the far west, extending toward the Atlantic Ocean. The first ruler to establish a state there was Qayamagha, the seat of his sovereignty being Ghana, a large city in the land of Baghana. It is said that the state (saltana) was founded by the Prophet Muhammad's mission, and that twenty-two kings ruled before that event, and twenty-two after, making a total of forty-four in all.

They were bidan in origin, though we do not know from whom they were originally descended - and their vassals (khuddam) were Soninke (Wa'kuriyyun). When their dynasty came to an end, they were succeeded by the Malians, who belong to the Sudan." (Hunwick 2003:14) The word literally means 'white people' according to Hunwick, the term is used in the western Sahara and Timbuktu region, and "the term has cultural rather than skin color connotations, and stands in opposition to the term Sudan - black people." (Hunwick 2003:13-14) Now, if we analyze the words of Hunwick as well as Al-sa'di's meaning regarding Bidan does not refer to one's skin tone only to one's culture in a region where blacks populate the land.

It would be fair to separate one person from another based on cultural identity and not make the mistake of arguing over race, which would be based on the grounds of a social construct created by racist a hundred plus years ago. So what is the significance of 'White Rule in West Afrika' so many questions remain? Who civilized West Afrikans? Where did they come from? And what evidence do we have to verify this claim? This makes al-Hasan b Muhammad al-Wazzan al-Zayyati account about West Africa worth our attention. Before we speak of his account, we need to understand a few things: who is al-Hasan b Muhammad al-Wazzan al-Zayyati, and did he originate this claim, or was it just accepted by Muslim scholars who carried this belief?

Who is al-Hasan b Muhammad al-Wazzan al-Zayyati?

"Leo Africanus was born al-Hasan b Muhammad al-Wazzan al-Zayyati, into a Muslim family of Granada that moved to Fez in the wake of the Christian Reconquista. At the age of 17 (sometime between 1506 and 1510), he accompanied his uncle on a diplomatic mission to Songhay and may have made another journey a few years later. In 1518, on his return from a visit to Egypt (possibly also Istanbul), and a pilgrimage to Mecca, he was captured by Sicilian corsairs and subsequently presented to Pope Leo X. Within a year, the pope had baptized him and given him the name, Johannis Leo de Medicis, the latter element of which was dropped in favor of the name Africanus. He stayed in Italy and wrote his Description of Africa, an Arabic-Hebrew-Latin vocabulary, and a treatise on prosody. He also taught Arabic at the University of Bologna. It is uncertain whether he died in Italy or returned to North Africa." (Hunwick 2003:272)

This information is important because we have to identify and understand the perspective of the Leo Africanus and his influence on scholarship in Africa but specifically West Africa. He is known for his publication titled the Description which Hunwick writes: 'he completed in 1526, was first published in Italian in 1550, and was soon translated into French, Latin, and English. Its principal focus is Mediterranean Africa, but it also contains a description of parts of the Sahara and the West African Sahel.' But what I find interesting is what Hunwick says next: 'While we have little reason to doubt that his descriptions of Timbuktu and Songhay are based on personal observation, recent scholarship has thrown doubt on his claim to have visited Hausa land and Bornu, suggesting that he gained his information from other travelers while in Gao or Agades. This does not necessarily invalidate the information he provides, though his accounts must be read more critically. One must also bear in mind that he was at least aware of al-Bakri's eleventh-century account of West Africa and had probably read it, and perhaps the account of al-Idrisi written in the following century. It is apparent that he sometimes drew upon these writers for geographical information (e.g., about the River Niger/ Nil), and perhaps supplemented his personal observations with material of theirs.' (Hunwick 2003:272-273)

So could Leo Africanus accounts be based on someone else's perspective, or did he formulate his own opinions of Bilad al Sudan and passed them off as if he bears witness to who actually ruled West Afrika? Let's review his observation word for word from his perspective to get a proper understand of his words: "The ancient geographers, such was al-Bakri and al-Mas'udi, wrote nothing about the Land of the Blacks, except for El Guichet and Gana. In fact, in their days, nothing was known about the lands of the Negroes. But they were discovered after the year 380 of the Hijra, because then the Lamtuna and all the population of Libya became Muslims, thanks to the propaganda of a preacher, who, in addition, pushed the Lamtuna to conquer the whole of Barbary. Then people began to visit these lands and to get to know them.

They are all inhabited by men who live like beast, without kings, lords, republics, governments, or customs. They hardly know how to sow grain. They dress in sheepskin. None of them has a wife of his own, who belongs to him alone. During the day, they graze cattle or work the soil; by night, ten or twelve men and women share a hut, and each one sleeps with the one who pleases him most, resting and sleeping on sheepskins." (Hunwick 2003:273-274)

Based on the description given above, it is safe to say that Leo Africanus has a very negative perspective of blacks in West Afrika, and it frustrates him at the way they behave and carry themselves differently from what he may be used to. As he continues: "No one makes war on anyone, and no one steps outside his territory. Some worship the sun and prostrate when they see it rising above the horizon. Others, such as the people of Walata, worship fire. Yet others are Christians, in the style of the Egyptians; such is the case of the people of the region of Gaogao. Joseph, the king and founder of Marrakesh, and the five people of Libya gained the power of these Blacks and taught them the Muslim law and what was necessary for them to lead their lives. Many became Muslims. It was then that Barbary merchants began to visit these lands to trade in different types of merchandise - so much so that they learned their languages. The five peoples of Libya divided up these lands among themselves, and each of these peoples of Libya had three of these parts. It is true that the present king of Timbuktu, Abu Baker Asia Izchia, is of the black race. He had been named captain-general of Sunni Ali (Suni Heli), king of Timbuktu and Gao, and of Libyan origin." (Hunwick 2003:274-275)

Here we have identified that foreigners from a distant land traveled to West Africa freely and civilized the negroes and taught them the Muslim way. How ironic that tribal people wouldn't make war with one another and chose to live peacefully within the confines of their territory.

These boring blacks who worshipped the sun, fire, and other things not living according to the perspective of others had to be saved by five Libyans who all ruled three parts of the land and brought fortune, fame, and excitement to West Afrika.

He continues: "After the death of Sunni Ali, Abu Baker revolted against his sons and put them to death. Then he delivered all the black people from the hands of the chiefs of those Libyan tribes, so effectively that he conquered several kingdoms in six years. When he had made his kingdom peaceful and secure, he felt a desire to go on pilgrimage to Mecca. In the course of this pilgrimage, he spent all his treasure and incurred 50,000 ducats of debt." (Hunwick 2003:274) Could the storylines of this new king be blurred and infused with that of another King from West Afrika? Hunwick seems to think so due to a lot of uncertainty that Leo Africanus has provided. 'Hamani (1989) argues that he (Leo Africanus) did not visit Agades. It is also highly unlikely that he visited Jenne or Mali.' (Hunwick 2003:272)

Hunwick writes: 'Leo thinks of the askiya of Songhay as king of Timbuktu and Gao. In his day, the 'king' was Askiya al-hajj Muhammad. It was his father who was called Abu Baker, which was also the name of last of the Sunni rulers whom he overthrew.' (Hunwick 2003:275) Africanus seems to be very confused about West Afrikan history and unaware of who ruled and when based on his account of a revolt and who was involved.

Africanus continues: "These fifteen kingdoms known to us stretch along the two banks of the Niger and its tributaries. They are situated between two immense deserts, one of which begins in Numidia and ends in these lands, while the other begins to the South and goes down to the ocean. There are numerous regions there, but most are unknown to us, either because of the length and difficulty of the journey or because of the diversity of languages and beliefs, which hinders them from having relations with the countries that are known to us, just as they hinder ours from having relations with theirs. However, some relations exist with

the Blacks who live on the ocean coast."
(Hunwick 2003:275)

Leo Africanus Accounts of 15 West Afrikan Kingdoms (word for word) source: Hunwick 2003:275-291

Kingdom of Walata: This small kingdom, and of mediocre condition compared to the other kingdoms of the blacks. In fact, the only inhabited places are three large villages, and some huts spread about among the palm groves. These villages are about three hundred miles south of Nun, about five hundred miles north of Timbuktu, and a hundred miles from the Atlantic Ocean. When the Libyan peoples dominated the region, they established their seat of royal government, and as a result, many Barbary merchants were accustomed to go there. But since the time of Sunni Ali, the merchants have little by little abandoned Walāta and have gone to Timbuktu and Gao, to such an extent that chief of Walata has become poor and powerless.

- The people of this land speak a language called Songhay.
- They are extremely black and lowly but very kind, especially towards strangers.
- The way of life and customs of the people of Walata are the same as those of their neighbors who inhabit the desert.
- Both men and women customarily cover their faces.
- These people live in the greatest misery and poverty.

Kingdom of Jenne: called Gheneoa by African merchants, by its people of Genni, and by the Portuguese and those who know these lands in Europe, Ghinea. It borders the preceding kingdom. However, there is a distance of about five hundred miles between the two across a desert. Walata is situated to the North, Timbuktu to the East, and Mali to the South. It stretches along the Niger for about two hundred and fifty miles, and one part of it is on the ocean, at the point where the Niger empties into the sea.

- There is neither a town nor a fortress; only a large village inhabited by the ruler, the priest, doctors, merchants, and the elite.
- All the houses these people live in are constructed like huts, roughcast with clay, and roofed with straw.
- The people of this village are very well dressed.
- The kingdom was formally governed by a family originating from the people of Libya, but during the time of Sunni Ali, the chief of this kingdom became tributary to him.

Kingdom of Mali: stretches along a branch of the Niger for a distance of perhaps three hundred miles. It borders on the preceding kingdom in the North and the South on a desert with arid mountains. In the West, its limits are primitive forests that stretch the ocean, while in the East it borders the territory of Gao. In this country, there is a very large village of nearly six thousand homes, which is called Mali. It is from this village that the whole kingdom takes its name. The king and the court live there.

- The inhabitants are rich on account of their trade, as they furnish Ghana and Timbuktu with many products.
- They have several temples, priests, and professors who teach in the temples since there are no colleges.
- They are the most civilized, the most intelligent, and most highly regarded of all the Blacks.
- At the time of their conversion, they were governed by the greatest of the princes of Libya, the uncle of Joseph, king of Marrakesh.

Kingdom of Timbuktu: The name of this kingdom is modern. It is that of a town which was built by a king called Mansa Sulayman in the year of the Hijra, at about twelve miles from a branch of the Niger. The houses of Timbuktu are huts made of stakes daubed with clay, and with straw roofs. In the middle of the town, there is a temple built with masoned stones and limestone mortar by an architect of the Beticos, a native of the town of al-Mana, and a large palace built by the same master builder, where the king stays. There are numerous artisans' workshops, merchants, and particular, weavers of cotton cloths. The cloths of Europe reach Timbuktu, brought by Barbary merchants.

- The women of the town still have the custom of veiling their faces, except for the slaves, who sell all the foodstuffs.
- The inhabitants are very rich, especially the resident strangers, to the extent that the present king has given two of his daughters in marriage to two merchant brothers, because of their wealth.
- The royal court is very well organized and magnificent.
- Many manuscript books coming from Barbary are sold.
- The people of Timbuktu have a light-hearted nature.

Kabara Town is a large town that looks like an unwalled village. It is twelve miles from Timbuktu, on the Niger. It is from there that merchants load merchandise to go to Jenne and Mali. The houses and inhabitants are like those that we have just spoken of. One finds their blacks of different races because it is the port to which they come from different regions with their canoes.

- At the time when I was in Kabara, this lieutenant was a relative of the king of Abu Baker and surnamed Pargama. He was a black man, though of great value because of his intelligence, and was very just.
- What is very injurious here is the frequent illnesses caused by the large quantities of food that are consumed - fish, milk, butter, and meat, all mixed.

Kingdom of Gao: is a very large town similar to the preceding one (Kabara), that is to say, without a surrounding wall. It is about four hundred miles south-east of Timbuktu. Its houses are general very ugly. However, there are a few very fine appearances where the king and his courts live. The town's inhabitants are rich merchants who continually roam around the region. Huge numbers of blacks go there taking large quantities of gold to buy items imported from Barbary and Europe, but they never find enough items to spend their gold, and they always take a half or two-thirds of it back home with them. The town is very civilized compared to Timbuktu.

- There is a square where on market days, huge numbers of slaves are sold, both male and female. A young girl of fifteen is worth about six ducats, and a young man almost as much; small children are worth about half as much as grown slaves.
- In fact, a horse worth ten ducats in Europe is here sold for forty or fifty.
- The remainder of the kingdom is made up of towns and villages, where cultivators and herdsmen live.
- In the winter, they dress in sheepskins. In summer, they go naked and barefoot.
- However, they cover up their shameful parts with a small rag and sometimes protected the soles of their feet with sandals of camel skin.
- These are men of total ignorance. You can scarcely find one who can read and write in the space of a hundred miles.

Kingdom of Gobir: This kingdom is some three hundred miles east of that of Gao. Between the two kingdoms, one crosses a desert where little water is to be found since it is forty miles from the Niger. This kingdom is situated between very high mountains. It contains a considerable number of villages inhabited by shepherds and cowherds. In fact, there is a large number of sheep and cattle, but of small size. The people are, in general, very civilized.

- It is inhabited by merchants, both local and foreign. Formerly, the king's residence and his court were in this location.
- The population is weighed down by taxes.
- Formerly it made large commercial profits; today, it is impoverished and reduced by more than half because Askiya has taken away from the country a very large number of men, keeping some of them captive and making others slaves.

The Kingdom of Agades is a walled town built by kings of the modern age on the borders of Libya. It is the town of Blacks closest to the towns of Whites, except for Walata. Its houses are very well constructed, after the manner of the houses of Barbary, because almost all the inhabitants are foreign merchants. There are very few local people, and these few Blacks are nearly all artisans or soldiers of the town's king. Each merchant owns a great number of slaves to serve as his escort on the road to Kano or Borno, for these routes are previously spoken of. There is an independent king in this land, but he was killed by Askiya, who also declared himself ruler of this kingdom.

Zamfara: is a region adjoining the latter one in the East. It is inhabited by several bases and crude peoples. The country has abundant grain, rice, millet, and cotton. The people of Zamfara are tall, but they are black beyond description, with long brutish faces more animal-like than human. Askiya poisoned their king and killed a large part of the people.

Kingdom of Guangara: This is a region that adjoins the preceding one towards the southeast. It is inhabited by a great people who could have seven thousand foot soldiers armed with bows and five hundred foreign cavalries. He obtains considerable revenue from merchandise and taxes on commerce. All the inhabited places are villages of straw huts, except one, which is bigger and more beautiful than the rest. The inhabitants are very rich because they go with their merchandise to distant lands, and because in a southerly direction, they are in the neighborhood of the land where large quantities of gold are found. Today, however, these people can undertake no foreign trade, because they have two cruel and powerful enemies: Askiya in the West, and the king of Bornu in the East. When I was in Bornu, the king of the country, Habraam, gathered together his entire army to go and attack the king of Guangara. But when he got close to that kingdom, he learned that Homara (Umar), the lord of Gaoga, was preparing to march on Bornu, so he immediately abandoned the enterprise to return to his kingdom with all speed. This was a great piece of good fortune for the king of Guangara.

The Kingdom of Bornu is a large province which borders Guangara in the West and stretches eastwards for about five hundred miles. It is about one hundred and fifty miles from the source of the Niger. In the south, it borders the desert of Set. In the North, it borders the deserts that are linked to Barca. This province has a variety of environments. Some regions are mountainous, and others consist of plains. In the plains, there are numerous villages inhabited by civilized folk and foreign merchants, both black and white. In the largest of these villages lives the king with his soldiers.

- The Mountain is peopled by shepherds who herd goats and oxen.
- These are men who have no religion, neither Christianity, Judaism, or Islam, but are without religious faith like beasts.
- They hold women and children in common. According to what I have heard said by a merchant who has lived in the three-country and

- understands its language, these people do not have proper names like people have elsewhere.
- The province is governed by a very powerful lord belonging to the Bardoa, a people in Libya.
- The king has no revenue other than what he obtains from raiding and killing his neighbors, who are his enemies.
- When I went to this kingdom, I found several desperate merchants who wanted to abandon this trade and never come back again, since they had been waiting there for a year without being paid.

These are the accounts of Leo Africanus not exaggerated or infused. Africanus speaks as an eyewitness who traveled the Bilad al-Sudan. He documented what he wrote, and he engaged in conversations with merchants along his way. What he did not like, he clearly states it, and when he felt the need to give credit to Libyans, he expressed it dearly. When he describes the blacks, he generalizes it as if the people are unbearable to look at similar to the racial descriptions of

Afrikan Americans during the minstrel movements, which made a mockery out of Blacks. Africanus is not alone in these thoughts about the Bidan: "Authors like Delafosse, Palmer, and Urvoy, who have provided much of our knowledge about the people of the Sudan, deliberately adopt this diffusionist standpoint." (Medeiros 1988:63)

What seems to be driving this generalization that Blacks aren't able to be civilized or created greatness is religious zealots whose agenda is to undermine Blacks in history. "While we are indebted to Arab geographers and historians for their contribution to the knowledge of these regions, we cannot close our eyes to their limitations. None of the writers visited the Sudan before Ibn Battuta in the fourteenth century, and most of them collected their information from hearsay at places far away from the countries they described. Their accounts are, therefore, fragmentary and, moreover, they reflect the cultural bias of Muslim intellectuals." (Medeiros 1988:64)

While reviewing information from Muslim intellectuals, we tend to not only witness biases but their influence on more recent scholarship. However, 'It was not until al-Idrisi that the theme of white origins was developed; this theme accordingly falls into the context of growing expansion of Islam in the Sudan.' (Medeiros 1988:70) Does this make al-Idrisi correct? No, because outside of him, what evidence exists that the Bidan is responsible for creating kingdoms? When Muslims made their way into the Sudan they came across a people who had already developed kingdoms while others were making strides in that direction. Medeiros states: 'The kings of the Sudan showed great political skill in their relations with the Muslim world and with the culture of all the northern partners with whom they had dealings. They used to their advantage the abilities of the Muslims who frequented their states.' (Medeiros 1988:72) So the Muslims traveled to West Afrika frequently to do business with the Blacks, which would indicate some type of government and structure pre-existed before the coming of any Libyans.

But, there's more: "Historians of the colonial period were inclined to attribute the creation of the kingdoms of Sahel to nomad invaders from the North, of white origin and of a higher civilization. Maurice Delafosse postulated a migration of the so-called 'Judea-Syrians,' who wandered from Libya to Bornu or Air, and then westwards across the Savannah. To these white migrants, whom he also regarded as ancestors of the Fulbe, Delafosse ascribed the creation of at least two kingdoms: Ghana and Takrur. This and other hypotheses are based on fragmentary and inconclusive evidence and are derived from the (now obsolete) assumption that the people of the Sudan could not develop organized states themselves." (Levtzion 1973:4) Delafosse argues that it was two kingdoms created by the Bidan while Leo Africanus is under the impression that five Bidan created kingdoms in West Africa. This has to be the reason why Levtzion and Medeiros both state that this hypothesis is based on "Fragmentary and Inconclusive Evidence."

What seems to be more interesting is how Levtzion ends his argument: "In the middle of the seventeenth century the authors of Ta'rikh al-Sudan and Ta'rikh al-Fattash (al-

Sadi and Ib al-Mukhtar), recorded old sayings that the first kings of Ghana had been white and their subjects 'Wa'kore' (i.e., Soninke). Historical traditions recorded since the turn of the century among the Soninke repeat the claim that their ancestor was a white man, who had come from the East. It is significant, however, that none of the early Arabic sources before the twelfth century imply that the rulers of Ghana (or, for that matter, Songhay and Takrur) were, or had been in the past, other than black. al-Idrisi was the first to write that the king of Ghana, 'according to what is reported, belongs to the progeny of Salih b Abdullah b al-Hasan b al-Hasan b Ali b Abi Talib.' Yet al-Idrisi wrote after the Almoravids' conquest of Ghana and the Islamization of that kingdom. One is tempted to seek Islamic influence in the claim to white (often Arab or even sharifian) origin." (Levtzion 1973:4)

So, is Leo Africanus responsible for regurgitating DelaFosse or al-Idrisi, or did he also come to this same conclusion based on his discovery? To be more specific, some scholars have raised great questions about

Africanus travels. Modern historians have noticed when dealing with Leo Africanus chronology; he could not have been in certain places at certain times. He has confused empires and kings with one another and also city-states. Some say he even borrowed the work of other geographers to publish his world renown book Description of Africa, which scholars from around the world used as a source when it comes to Africa specifically.

Let's review some of Leo's fables or stories about himself and his journeys: A lot of doubt about Africanus life has led to some questions about his childhood and family. "Leo's contemporaries are so silent regarding him, that almost nothing is known as to his ways of life or character, beyond what can be gathered from the pages of his magnum opus. However, this is in many places so frankly autobiographical, that it is possible to piece together from various passages a fair picture of the man who was for nearly three centuries the sole authority on the geography of Northern and Central Africa." (aluka.org)

"According to the usual legend, Leo must have been seventeen or eighteen. This of course renders it impossible for us to accept 1491 as the year of his birth; and as Leo's personal acquaintance with "Sidi Jeja" did not begin till two years after the capitulation of Saffi, namely, in 1509, the difficulty of believing that he was born earlier than three or four years after the fall of the last Moorish kingdom in Spain becomes an impossibility. Who his father was, we are not told, except that he owned land, etc. But it is certain, from the distinguished position which his relatives occupied in Morocco, that he was a man of wealth and consequence, both in Fez, and previously in Granada. Leo's uncle seems also to have been a person of consequence; for he was sent as Ambassador from the King of. Fez to the King of Timbuktu, and bore a wide reputation as "an excellent Orator and a most wittie Poet." Leo seems also to have had another relative at Fez, who impoverished himself with the study of alchemy (p. 66); but beyond this, we know nothing of his family, and nearly all that we know of his career is derived from the incidental remarks he chooses to vouchsafe in the course of his work." (aluka.org)

Points of Contention with Leo's work: Hunwick, Aluka.org

- His account of Askia is wrong based on his account he gives us on Agadez and the conditions of the town as well as the date.
- He also repeats a lot of mistakes al-Idrisi makes on his accounts of the Niger Kingdoms.
- Africanus does not produce any accurate dates, especially for someone who speaks as if he's an eyewitness.
- Wangara was a Muslim state for more than 300 years.
- Africanus confuses Lake Chad with the Niger River.
- He has a lot of inaccuracies in his work when it comes to West Africa
- More modern scholars would argue that he deferred to other Muslim scholars regarding his work.
- Leo uses the name Libya for the Sahara in Descriptions of Africa pg.5

- North African merchants had been making trading journeys to do business since the 8th century.
- Leo confuses Askia of Songhai with a king of Timbuktu and Gao.
- No evidence exists regarding the people Jenne being the people of Libya.
- The Mali kingdom, from its inception, is the Malinke.
- Leo claims Mansa Sulayman built Timbuktu; his reign was in 1341 - 1360.
- Chronicles of Kano make no mention of any Songhai conquest.
- Leo's Niger seems to flow out of Lake Chad based on his account in his book.

In conclusion: The man of many names tends to bite off more than he can chew, and until recently, numerous scholars relied on his works as if they had been first-hand eyewitness accounts. Leo Africanus was heavily influenced by Muslim scholars who predated him and provided their own geographical and historical worldview on Africa in general, among other places. Are all his accounts not trustworthy I am not arguing that, because there are some things in his works he's right about, but the focus is on his initial claims of the Bidan rule in West Africa and the location these people that traveled from Libya to start these kingdoms, as well as his accounts that blacks were not civilized and or responsible for their success prior to the coming of Islam.

Even the earliest mentioning of Bidan by Al-Sa'di references us to a people who did not have a similar culture as those in Bilad al-Sudan. As shown throughout this chapter, it is very hard to trust his accounts regarding Bilad al-Sudan, because he tends to take a very racist approach when describing the people in each kingdom. His cultural biases make one wonder if he ever actually visited West Afrika and just relied on merchants as a source for his worldview. To a religious mind, one would deem a people pagan and uncivilized if they did not follow the path Mohammad or Jesus paved for them.

What's even more dangerous about Africanus accounts is that numerous African and African American scholars who have relied on his work as primary source and influence, and we haven't found many to challenge and correct his work. Understandably, some scholars did not have the necessary tools or reason to go behind Africanus and correct his work. Some scholars have appealed to authority, while others relied on more concrete evidence. Medieros, Hunwick, and Levtzion have spearheaded a movement to make sure that White Rule in West Africa was nothing more than a fairytale told by people who refused to accept the genius of Blacks in Africa.

"Ignorance can lead to potential danger. It is important to be informed and alert."
- West Afrikan Proverb

Overall

Before the Spread of Islam, Africans lived a heterogeneous way that allowed tribal people to define their natural world based on their current events. This understanding meant that within each clan and overall tribe, one could cultivate its traditional beliefs and practices that served a purpose among its people. Africans had little to nothing to do with the creation of Islam and its spread; they only became victimized by Islam from its onset due to the greed and havoc it wreaked upon the continent as it crept toward the Mediterranean.

Archeological evidence shows an early A.D. presence in the Horn of Africa due to the Red Sea trade. Still, Islam's cultural nuisances played no role in reshaping East African culture within the region. Knowledge of this only strengthens the argument that Islam's early presence help fuel its greed in the coming years after the Prophet deemed it necessary to military makes its power felt. As it crept from Arabia into Africa, jihad left a pool of blood and conversion that many sources seldom mention and reference.

Upon its approach toward Bilād al-Sūdān, Islam traveled through North Africa, converting and spreading the words of the Prophet. Muslims deemed this necessary, and due to external sources, the romanticism of Arabic culture swept across North Africa as it set its eyes on the 'Land of The Blacks.' Islam played the political game early on; it needed to because it was foreign to the land. As the Prophet once illustrated, magic was vital in the persuasion of an ignorant man. African ignorance of its neighbors made it easy prey. This behavior was seen throughout history as its heterogeneous way of life created division that continued to make it vulnerable. Muslims wanted the gold, the girls, and the glamour of building up an Arabic presence in a foreign land that would provide a pathway for its dominance forever in its eyes.

Jihad, trade, and slaves were tools used to refine the worldview of West Africans. Eliminate your traditions and beliefs and teach you new ones while playing a psychological game that continues to last. Today the majority of West Africans are

Muslim but cloaked in colonial confusion. Most of the children have no idea about its greatness, ancestral traditions, and more. Muslim romanticists in America, specifically the black community, play an apologist role in pushing this Afro-Asiatic ideology. They make unproven claims about who we are, and this pseudo-historical narrative supports a false dichotomy that none have yet to prove. These are the underlining issues with the overall enslavement of the Continental African and Diaspora Africans who struggle with identity.

Each chapter in this book represents the struggles we face as a people when we allow external sources to shape and mold all Africans minds and push an ideology on us that contradicts who we are. The conqueror won; yes, we can admit that, but we are not compelled to remain in the seat of a mental slave unless we are comfortable in that role. If we seriously believed that Allah had our best interest in our heart, why is so much blood on 'his' hands? Muhammad was not a prophet of the African people; he was a prophet to his Arabic followers, and this is the pill many of us are unwilling to swallow.

The Coming of Islam in Bilād al-Sūdān was no gentle introduction and inception, nor was its use of political and social prowess in a foreign land. Islam gained wealth while African nations suffered and where African countries thrived, Muslims controlled the overall narrative.

Traditional beliefs suffered from losing certain customs and beliefs that once had significant meaning to their people. Only the rich benefited from trade while everyone else had to work small, odd jobs to stay afloat. Arabs were the earliest racists to step foot on African soil; today, people act as if those same Arabs prejudices died. The short answer to that is not we can look at the behavior of the Berbers and Arabs in Morocco toward the Sudanic Africans.

Lastly, there was nothing merciful or benevolent about Islam in West Africa. People have tried to justify it as such, but it did more harm than good, and when we assess the overall effects, Islam's role in West Africa will keep it underdeveloped in the coming years.

Sources

Introduction

- Ibn-Ḫaldūn Yaḥya Ibn-Muḥammad, et al. The Muqaddimah. Univ. Press, 1967.

Chapter Two

- Hunwick, John O. West Africa, Islam and the Arab World: Essays in Honour of Basil Davidson. Markus Wiener Publishers, 2006.

- Hopkins, J.F.P, and Nehemia Levtzion. Corpus of Early Arabic Sources for West African History. Cambridge University Press, 1981.

- Crowder, Michael. West Africa: an Introduction to Its History. Longman, 1990.

- Azumah, John Alembillah. The Legacy of Arab-Islam in Africa: a Quest for Inter-Religious Dialogue. Oneworld, 2016.

- Elfasi, M., and I. Hrbek. General History of Africa. III, Africa from the Seventh to the Eleventh Century. Abridged ed., III, Heinemann Educational, 1992.

- Akyeampong, Emmanuel Kwaku. Themes in West Africa's History. Ohio University Press, 2016.

- Insoll, Timothy. The Archaeology of Islam in Sub-Saharan Africa. Cambridge University Press, 2003.

- Saad, Elias N. Social History of Timbuktu: the Role of Muslim Scholars and Notables, 1400-1900. Cambridge University Press, 2010.

Chapter Three

- Ragil, Robert. "Contextualizing Jihad and Takfir in the Sunni Conceptual Framework." The Washington Institute, 2018, www.washingtoninstitute.org/policy-analysis/contextualizing-jihad-and-takfir-sunni-conceptual-framework.

- Insoll, Timothy. The Archaeology of Islam in Sub-Saharan Africa. Cambridge University Press, 2003.

- Ade., Ajayi Jacob F. Slavery and Slave Trade in Nigeria: from Earliest Times to the Nineteenth Century. Safari Books, 2010.

- Ibn-Ḫaldūn Yaḥya Ibn-Muḥammad, et al. The Muqaddimah. Univ. Press, 1967.

- Hunwick, John O. West Africa, Islam and the Arab World: Essays in Honour of Basil Davidson. Markus Wiener Publishers, 2006.

- Hunwick, John O., and Eve Troutt Powell. The African Diaspora in the Mediterranean Lands of Islam. Markus Wiener, 2010.

- Azumah, John Alembillah. The Legacy of Arab-Islam in Africa: a Quest for Inter-Religious Dialogue. Oneworld, 2016.

Chapter Four

- Gomez, Michael A. African Dominion: a New History of Empire in Early and Medieval West Africa. Princeton University Press, 2019.

- Hall, Bruce S. A History of Race in Muslim West Africa: 1600-1960. Cambridge University Press, 2011.

- Hopkins, J.F.P, and Nehemia Levtzion. Corpus of Early Arabic Sources for West African History. Cambridge University Press, 1981.

- Hunwick, John O. West Africa, Islam and the Arab World: Essays in Honour of Basil Davidson. Markus Wiener Publishers, 2006.

- Hunwick, John O., and Eve Troutt Powell. The African Diaspora in the Mediterranean Lands of Islam. Markus Wiener, 2010.

- Elfasi, M., and I. Hrbek. General History of Africa. III, Africa from the Seventh to the Eleventh Century. Abridged ed., III, Heinemann Educational, 1992.

- Health, National Institute of. "Race." Genome.gov, National Human Genome Research Institute, 2020, www.genome.gov/genetics-glossary/Race.

Chapter Five

- Piesie, Kofi, et al. From Spears to Pens. II, Kofi Piesie Reasearch Team, 2020.

- Ade, Ajayi Jacob Festus, and Michael Crowder. History of West Africa. Volume One. Vol. 1, Longman, 1976.

- Boahen, A. Adu, and Alvin M. Josephy. The Horizon History of Africa. American Heritage Pub. Co., 1971.

- Elfasi, M., and I. Hrbek. General History of Africa. III, Africa from the Seventh to the Eleventh Century. Abridged ed., III, Heinemann Educational, 1992.

- Hunwick, John O. West Africa, Islam and the Arab World: Essays in Honour of Basil Davidson. Markus Wiener Publishers, 2006.

- Ibn-Ḫaldūn Yaḥya Ibn-Muḥammad, et al. The Muqaddimah. Univ. Press, 1967.

- Insoll, Timothy. The Archaeology of Islam in Sub-Saharan Africa. Cambridge University Press, 2003.

Chapter Six

- Ade, Ajayi J F, and Ian Espie. A Thousand Years of West African History. Humanity Press, 1967.

- Ade, Ajayi Jacob Festus, and Michael Crowder. History of West Africa. Volume One. Vol. 1, Longman, 1976.

- Austen, Ralph A. Trans-Saharan Africa in World History. Oxford University Press, 2010.

- Davidson, Basil, et al. A History of West Africa to the Nineteenth Century. With F.K. Buah and the Advice of J.F. Ade Ajayi. Longmans, 1967.

- Elfasi, M., and I. Hrbek. General History of Africa. III, Africa from the Seventh to the Eleventh Century. Abridged ed., III, Heinemann Educational, 1992.

- Niane, D T, and J KI-Zerbo. General History of Africa. Abridged ed., IV, UNESCO, 1997.

Chapter Seven

- Ajayi, Jacob Festus Ade, and Michael Crowder. History of West Africa. Volume One. Longman, 1976.

- Africanus, Leo. "The History and Description of Africa and of the Notable Things Therein Contained, Vol. 1." The History and Description of Africa and of the Notable Things Therein Contained, Vol. 1, Jstor&Aluka, 1896, psimg.jstor.org/fsi/img/pdf/t0/10.5555/al.ch.document.nuhmafricanus1_final.pdf.

- Wei-Haas, Maya. "First Ancient Genomes from West Africa Reveal Complexity of Human Ancestry." National Geographic, National Geographic, 24 Jan. 2020, www.nationalgeographic.com/science/2020/01/first-ancient-genomes-west-africa-complexity-human-ancestry/.Zimmer, Carl.

- "Ghost DNA Hints at Africa's Missing Ancient Humans." Ghost Dna Hints at Africa, Google, 12 Feb. 2020, www.google.com/amp/s/www.nytimes.com/2020/02/12/science/west-africa-ancient-humans.amp.html.

- Ackerley, Bethan. "DNA Analysis of People in West Africa Reveals 'Ghost' Human Ancestor." New Scientist, 12 Feb. 2020, www.newscientist.com/article/2233488-dna-analysis-of-people-in-west-africa-reveals-ghost-human-ancestor/.Hopkins, J.F.P, and Nehemia Levtzion.

- Corpus of Early Arabic Sources for West African History. Cambridge University Press, 1981.

- Ajayi, J. F. Ade., and Ian Espie. A Thousand Years of West African History. Humanities, 1972.

- Fāsī Muḥammad, and Ivan Hrbek. Africa from the Seventh to the Eleventh Century. Vol. 3, Heinemann Educational Books, 1988.

- Levtzion, Nehemia. Ancient Ghana and Mali. S.n., 1973.

- Saʻdī, ʻAbd al-Raḥmān ibn ʻAbd Allāh Sa'di, and John O. Hunwick. Timbuktu and the Songhay Empire: Al-Sa'dī's Ta'rīkh Al-sūdān down to 1613 and Other Contemporary Documents. Brill, 2003.

- HUNWICK, JOHN O. "A REGION OF THE MIND: MEDIEVAL ARAB VIEWS OF AFRICAN GEOGRAPHY AND ETHNOGRAPHY AND THEIR LEGACY." Sudanic Africa, vol. 16, 2005, pp. 103–136. JSTOR, www.jstor.org/stable/25653429. Accessed 17 May 2020.

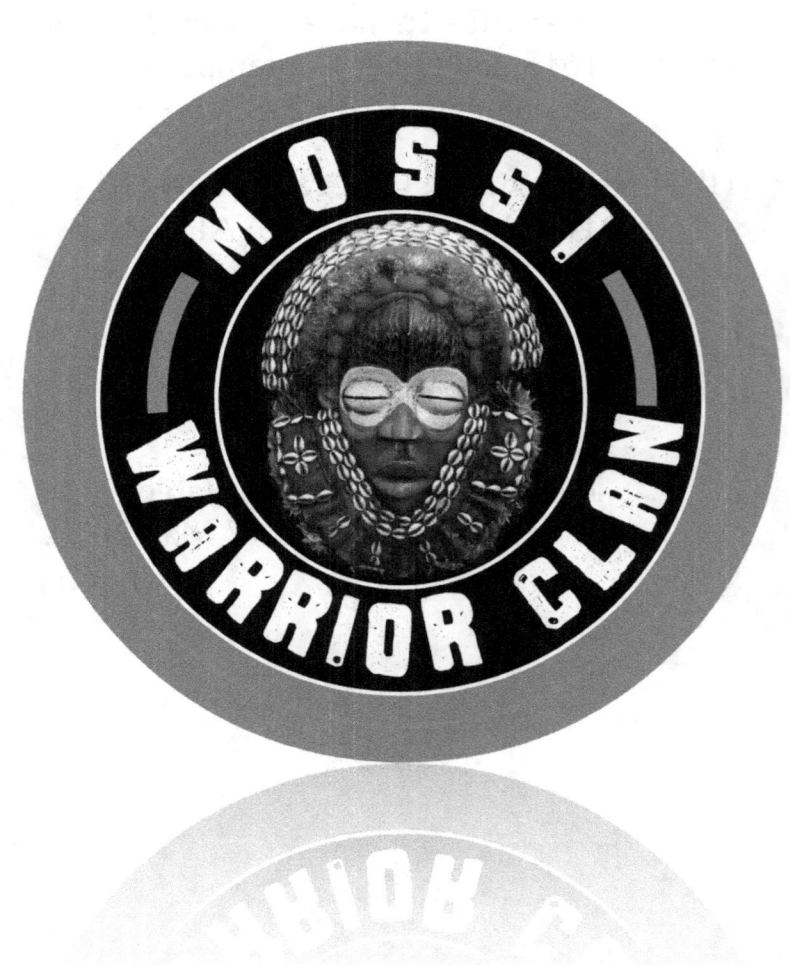

Mossi Warrior Clan Presents

From Cocaine to Consciousness

By Ini-Herit Khalfani

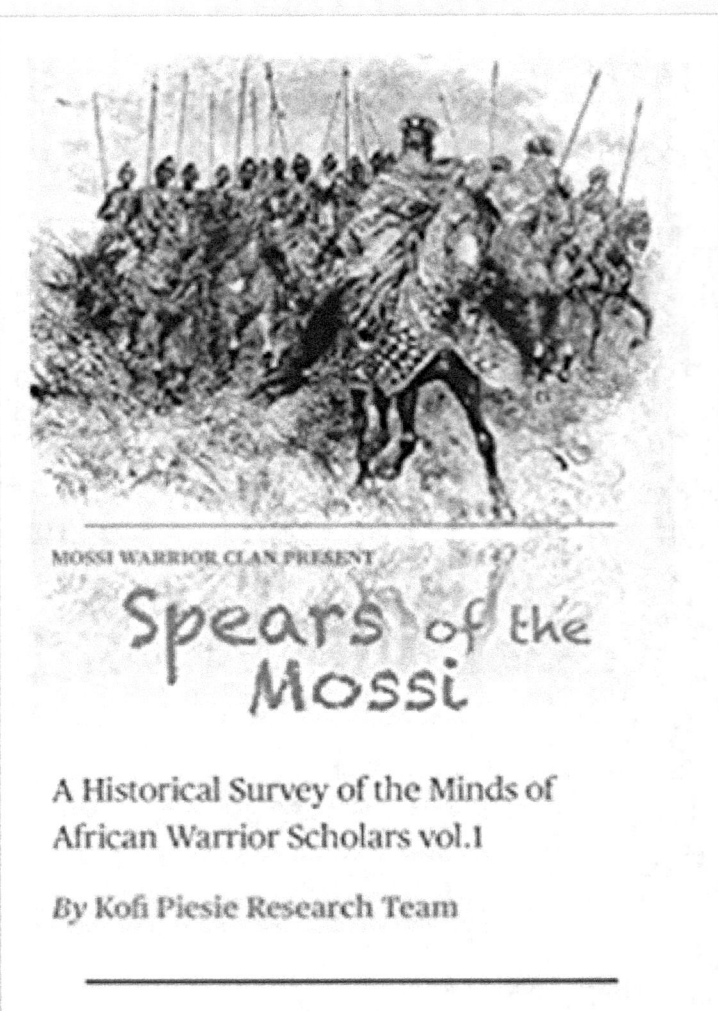

MOSSI WARRIOR CLAN PRESENT

Spears of the Mossi

A Historical Survey of the Minds of African Warrior Scholars vol.1

By Kofi Piesie Research Team

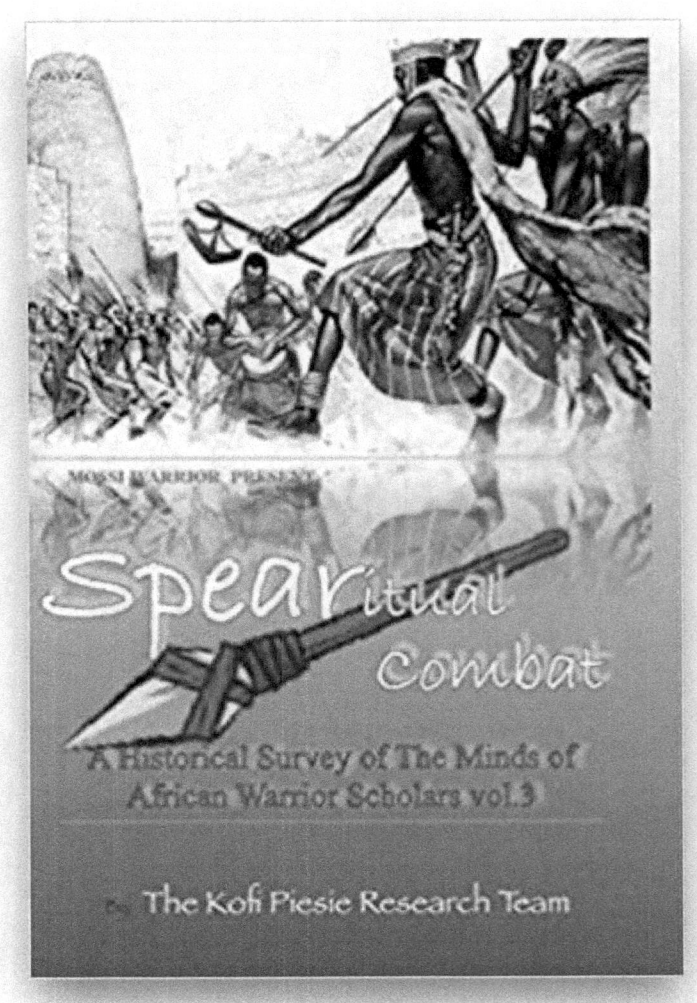

www.ingramcontent.com/pod-product-compliance
Lightning Source LLC
Chambersburg PA
CBHW060953230426
43665CB00015B/2184